Alexander Maclaren

The conquering Christ and other sermons

Alexander Maclaren

The conquering Christ and other sermons

ISBN/EAN: 9783743300125

Manufactured in Europe, USA, Canada, Australia, Japa

Cover: Foto ©ninafisch / pixelio.de

Manufactured and distributed by brebook publishing software (www.brebook.com)

Alexander Maclaren

The conquering Christ and other sermons

CONQUERING CHRIST

AND

OTHER SERMONS

BY

ALEXANDER MACLAREN, D.D.

NEW YORK
E. P. DUTTON & CO.
31, WEST TWENTY-THIRD STREET
1891

LONDON:
PRINTED BY WILLIAM CLOWES AND SONS, LIMITED,
STAMFORD STREET AND CHARING CROSS.

CONTENTS.

THE CONQUERING CHRIST.

"Behold the Lamb of God, which taketh away the sin of the world!"—JOHN i. 29.
"And I beheld, and, lo, . . . a Lamb as it had been slain."—REV. v. 6 1

SPOKEN NEED, UNSPOKEN REQUEST.

"And when they wanted wine, the mother of Jesus saith unto Him, They have no wine."—JOHN ii. 3.
"Therefore his sisters sent unto Jesus, saying, Lord, behold, he whom Thou lovest is sick."—JOHN xi. 3 ... 19

GLIMPSES OF THE HEART OF JESUS.

"Being moved with compassion, He stretched forth His hand."—MARK i. 41 33

GATHERED IN PEACE.

"Behold, I will gather thee to thy fathers, and thou shalt be gathered to thy grave in peace."—2 CHRON. xxxiv. 28.
"The archers shot at King Josiah; and the king said unto his servants, Have me away; for I am sore wounded. . . . And they brought him to Jerusalem, and he died."—2 CHRON. xxxv. 23, 24 51

SOME REASONS WHY THE WORD BECAME FLESH.

"He is not ashamed to call them brethren, saying, I will declare Thy name unto My brethren, in the midst of the Church will I sing praise to Thee. And again, I will put My trust in Him. And again, Behold I and the children which God hath given Me."—HEB. ii. 11-13 67

ARMED RECREANTS.

"The children of Ephraim, being armed, and carrying bows, turned back in the day of battle."—Ps. lxxviii. 9 ... 83

"AN INCREASING PURPOSE."

"These all, having had witness borne to them through their faith, received not the promise, God having provided some better thing concerning us, that they without us should not be made perfect."—HEB. xi. 39, 40 (R.V.) 93

THE DEFENCE OF THE DEFENCELESS.

"A land of unwalled villages . . . them that are at rest, that dwell safely, all of them dwelling without walls, and having neither bars nor gates."—EZEK. xxxviii. 11.
"Jerusalem shall be inhabited as towns without walls. . . . For I, saith the Lord, will be unto her a wall of fire round about, and will be the glory in the midst of her."—ZECH. ii. 4, 5 ... 109

HOW A CHURCH LIVES AND GROWS.

"From whom the whole body, by joints and bands having nourishment ministered and knit together, increaseth with the increase of God."—COL. ii. 19 121

WISE HASTE.

"See that ye hasten the matter."—2 CHRON. xxiv. 5. 137

PHASES OF FAITH.

"Many believed on Him. Then said Jesus to those Jews which believed on Him . . ."—JOHN viii. 30, 31 147

TENT AND ALTAR.

"Abram pitched his tent, . . . and there he builded an altar."
—GEN. xii. 8 161

THE FORGIVING SON OF MAN.

"That ye may know that the Son of man hath power on earth to forgive sins, (then saith He to the sick of the palsy,) Arise, take up thy bed, and go unto thine house."—MATT. ix. 6 ... 173

CHRIST'S "VERILY, VERILY."

"Verily, verily, I say unto you."—JOHN i. 51 189

THE CONQUERING CHRIST.

THE CONQUERING CHRIST.

"Behold the Lamb of God, which taketh away the sin of the world!"—JOHN i. 29.

"And I beheld, and, lo, . . . a Lamb as it had been slain."—REV. v. 6.

ONE of the disciples of the Baptist who heard his proclamation of the Lamb of God was John, afterwards the apostle and writer of the Apocalypse. Long years had passed since that hour. The Baptist slept in a bloody grave. The young fisherman had learned to know Jesus with a larger knowledge, and to love Him with a love more than life. He had found in Jesus depths which he had little dreamed of, on that day by the fords of Jordan; and now, in his rocky Patmos, with the waves dashing round him, in a scene so unlike the earlier one, and himself most changed of all, the heavens were opened, and the vision of his Lord granted to him again. Is it not beautiful and significant that the words in which he tells of what he saw through the door opened in heaven, read like an echo of those spoken so long ago, and never to be forgotten?—"Behold the Lamb!" "And I beheld, and, lo, . . . a Lamb!" The word for *lamb* is, indeed, different, and in the difference lies a pathetic and lovely lesson; for that employed to describe the heavenly state of the exalted Christ is humbler than that used by the Baptist, being a diminutive form, which we might represent by *lambkin*. But the whole ring of the sentence is like that of the original proclamation in the Gospel. If we further notice that the fourth Gospel alone has preserved this testimony of the forerunner, and that John alone of New Testament writers uses this name for Christ, and that it occurs in the Apocalypse some twenty-five times, we see how deeply his first teacher's words had sunk into his heart, and how constantly, as years advanced and his experience widened, he had found them assuming new meaning. Happy is it for us if life but reveals to us the fulness which lies in our earliest glimpses of Christ, if our old age can repeat the creed of youth with deepened significance, and if we can hope that heaven itself will but give us a clearer vision of the same Christ, in the same character as we had dimly seen Him amid the confusions and sorrows of earth!

The purpose of this sermon is to gather into one view the Apocalyptic uses of this name for Jesus Christ, and thus to try to bring out the remarkable fulness and variety of the representation of what Christ is to men, thence deducible. We may arrange the whole roughly in four classes, and consider the teaching of the Apocalypse as to the slain Lamb, the enthroned Lamb, the Shepherd-Lamb, and the Warrior-Lamb.

I. We have first the representation given in the words of our second text—the slain Lamb, the Sin-bearer for the world.

If we recur for a moment to the testimony of the forerunner, and try to throw ourselves back to his standpoint, and to ask the meaning on his lips of that remarkable saying, we shall better understand the vision in Patmos.

The aspect in which Jesus appeared to the last of the Old Testament prophets was necessarily moulded by Old Testament facts, and if we seek what these may have been, we shall not go far wrong if we point to a triple source for that testimony of his, in the Lamb of history, the Lamb of ritual, and the Lamb of prophecy.

As for the first of these three, recall the pathetic question and answer which passed between Abraham and his son as they travelled to the mountain of sacrifice. "Where is the lamb for the burnt offering?" said the unconscious son, bearing the wood for the pile. "My son," said the father—and how hard it must have been to have steadied his voice to say it, and to look the confidence which he did not feel!—"God Himself will provide the lamb." The despairing father was "wiser than he knew," and the event shamed the little faith which he had in his own words. Surely that utterance, floating down from the sacred past, helped to shape the Baptist's speech, and the remembrance of it suggests the interpretation of the "Lamb of God," as being the Sacrifice appointed and provided by God Himself.

Further, a second source, confluent with the former, is the Lamb of ritual, whether the daily sacrifice or the Paschal lamb. In this connection it is to be noted that John in his Gospel lays stress on the fact that, by reason of the remarkable rapidity with which death followed our Lord's crucifixion, His sacred body escaped the cruel indignity practised on the two robbers to hasten their end. He sees therein the fulfilment of the prescription concerning the Paschal sacrifice, "a bone of it shall not be broken," and thus by that one passing allusion identifies Jesus with the Passover —an identification which is also distinctly asserted by our Lord in His institution of the Last Supper.

Further, we must take into account also, and perhaps chiefly, the Lamb of prophecy—the great picture of the meek and suffering Servant of the Lord in the second part of Isaiah. "He was led as a lamb to the slaughter, and as a sheep before her shearers is dumb, so He opened not His mouth." But not meekness only was predicated of this Sufferer, but also that in some mysterious fashion He should "bear our griefs and carry our sorrows," and that the Lord should "make to meet on Him the iniquity of us all." The coincidence of representation is too striking to be fortuitous; and the interpretation of the words of the Baptist, which takes no account of the words of the prophet, may be admired for its courage, but scarcely for its clear-sightedness.

If we give due weight to these three sources—history, ritual, and prophecy—we shall be shut up to the conclusion that the title given by the Baptist to Jesus is a name of function rather than of character. It is a transparently inadequate explanation to make the name a mere expression of meekness or of innocence. True, these qualities must and do attach to the Sacrifice which is to avail for men, but it is not these qualities, but the fact of sacrifice, which is insisted upon in the title. That is made certain as having been the Baptist's meaning by his own following words, which place the point of comparison between Jesus and "the lamb" in His sin-bearing rather than in His disposition. And how strong and emphatic the description of His mighty work is! He "taketh away" by taking on Himself. The burden is not "sins," but "sin;" as if all the black deeds were gathered into one huge mass, enough to crush any shoulders but His on whom it is laid. The universality of His work of bearing, and bearing away sin, is put in the strongest form by the addition—"of the world."

So far the Baptist carries us. John had heard and dimly understood his words. But much had happened since then to open their depths to his gaze. He had stood by the cross, had seen his risen Lord, had received His guiding Spirit, had learned through long years his own and the world's need, had pondered and prayed and preached and lived, and so had come to know how "the blood of Jesus Christ cleanseth from all sin." Therefore, with whatever sacrifice of congruity of metaphor, the vision which he sees when heaven opens is "a Lamb as it had been slain." Whatever may be said about other points of comparison as being present in the Baptist's use of the emblem, the sacrificial import of the vision in Revelation is settled by that one expression. "As it had been slain" leaves no doubt that Christ's death, and nothing else, is in the seer's mind; and that to that fact he would lead us as the centre-point of all else which we can know about Him, and as the foundation of all that He has further to reveal of His glory and power.

That symbolical representation is a vivid and picturesque way of saying that, in heaven as on earth, Christ's sacrifice is efficacious and necessary. Much besides may be contained in the symbol, but this is plainly its lesson, that there is no heaven nor any cleansing but through the blood of the slain Lamb. For earth and heaven, to the last moment of time and all through the dateless cycles of eternity, Christ's sacrifice is men's need, and is present before the throne as the medium of all blessings to sinners here who struggle to be saints, and to saints there who were sinners. Purity, peace, life, and all other Divine gifts, are ours and theirs, because the "Lamb as it had been slain" is before the throne. "This Man, when He had offered one sacrifice for sins for ever, sat down on the right hand of the throne of God."

This is the aspect of Christ with which we must begin, if we would know Him in the full greatness of His gifts and sweep of His work. Unless we do, we shall have but an unworthy conception of His wondrous love and an inadequate estimate of His all-healing power. The Christianity which strikes out the sacrifice on the cross from its idea of Jesus has not fathomed the depths of His mercy nor of our need. The wounds of humanity are not to be stanched by one who is but a meek and pure pattern man, however stimulating and lovable such a figure may be, but need for their binding up a wounded hand. A Christ without a cross is an impotent Christ. He can neither bless nor sway. It used to be believed that adamant was soluble only by the blood of a kid. The adamantine heart is melted by nothing else than by the sacrifice of that unblemished and spotless Lamb. Take away that figure from the vision of the future, and the vision itself melts into mist, and instead of the solid certainties of a real and accessible home of all blessedness and perfection, there remains but a great Perhaps, shimmering uncertainly in the vapour, and in our hearts the aching doubt of its reality and of our power to reach it, if real it be.

II. A second group of passages presents the enthroned Lamb.

The vision from which our second text comes shows the Lamb between the throne and the ring of worshippers, and in other places of the Apocalypse we read of "the Lamb in the midst of the throne," and, still more remarkably, of "the throne of God and of the Lamb," as if joint possessors of the one seat of majesty. These are but symbolical ways of proclaiming the truth that the cross leads to the crown, that the dominion of Jesus is founded upon His suffering and death, that the many crowns which He wears are His by right of His having worn the crown of thorns. That Divine Word, which became flesh for our sakes, returned to the glory which had been its home before the world was; but it bore a new companion with it—even the humanity which it assumed, and which died for our salvation. Manhood is exalted to the sovereign place in the universe. The slain Lamb is the enthroned Lamb. This vision brings clearly into view the activity of Jesus in His heavenly state, as well as His sovereign exaltation. For the ground plan of the universe is contained in it. In the centre rises the throne. Round it afar off are gathered the living creatures, the representatives of the fulness of creatural life; and the elders, the representatives of redeemed humanity; and between these and the throne stands the slain Lamb, through whom all communications between the throne and the worshippers pass. By Him all blessings flow out, and by Him all praise rises up. "By Him all things consist." By Him the creatures receive their meat according to their hunger and capacity. By Him redeemed manhood receives all its graces and hopes. He is the Channel of all good, and bestows all fulness on an else empty world. He is the Medium by which thanksgiving, devotion, aspiration, hope, dare to clasp the else inaccessible seat of God.

Nor is this the only thought enforced by the vision, for its subsequent part tells how this throned Lamb took into His hand the book with seven seals, and as He broke them one by one, set loose as it were the mighty forces which were to mould the world's destiny. Jesus Christ is the Lord of history. The hand that was pierced on the cross holds the helm. The voice which cried, "It is finished!" says to His servants, who ride upon the mysterious horses of the vision, "Go!" and they go on their errand of woe or gladness. He is the King of nations. Do we not see that, in spite of all the talk about Christ having done His part and Christianity being worn out, the principles and powers that spring from His cross are more and more becoming the guides of the "civilized" world? Much of the evidence of His rule is plain to all who are not blinded by antagonism and prejudice, and the fact of His rule should be the unalterable conviction of every Christian soul, for its own peace amid noisy rebellion. But we need purged eyes to see that great sight which John saw in Patmos.

It is of the utmost importance for the vigour of Christian life to keep clear and vivid that present activity of our Lord. We have not only to look back to His cross, but upwards to His throne. We have not only to rejoice that He was wounded for a world's transgressions, and to adore Him who was slain for us, but to think of Him as at the right hand of God, ready to help and royal to defend all who love Him. The nobleness, peacefulness, and strength of our lives largely depend upon our having that vision of the enthroned Jesus ever before us. It will give substance and nearness to the else shadowy and remote thoughts of heaven, if we feel that He is actually there in the manhood which is ours, and actually wielding the energies of omnipotence on behalf of our feebleness and for effecting the mighty purposes of His death. The distant land is more real and less distant when one dear vision fills it, and our Brother is known to be there. We shall have more vivid conceptions of Him, when our thoughts are not only directed to Him as to an historical figure in the past centuries, but embrace Him as at this moment working for the completion of that great work, which, though in one aspect it was "finished" when He bowed His head and died, in another will not be completed till the voice from heaven proclaims, "It is done. The kingdoms of this world are become the kingdom of our God and of His Christ."

It is difficult to keep that vision clear before our eyes, amid our low cares and sense-bound thinkings. But how small and poor the noise of Ephesus and the storms of persecution would seem to John, when the heavens opened and showed him the throned Christ! There is no reason why that sight should not bless us as really as it blessed him. He saw "the things that are," and they *are* to-day and for ever. It was no transient splendour which he saw, nor was he befooled by the phantasms of his own imagination. To him was granted but the Apocalypse or the unveiling of what was always there, behind the curtain. For us, too, it will be drawn back, if we will. It is but a thin separating veil, which will soon be rent asunder, and may at any time be drawn aside, for faithful eyes to gaze lovingly on the glories which it partially hides. How small cares, and sorrows, and joys, and aims of this life would look if we really saw, with the inward eye whose revelations are more trustworthy than those of sense, the enthroned Lamb, the Mediator of the fulness of God, and the Arbiter of the fates of men! If we would purge our vision from earthly stain, we too should have it granted to us to see this great sight, and to walk all the day in the light of the countenance of the present and exalted Christ.

III. Another group of passages gives the figure of the Shepherd-Lamb.

In that tender description of the perfected flock that

came out of great tribulation, which has solaced so many sad hearts with a glimpse of the blessedness of their dear ones gone, we read that "the Lamb which is in the midst of the throne shall shepherd them, and shall guide them unto fountains of waters of life;" and in another vision we hear of the redeemed as "following the Lamb whithersoever He goeth." Of course the colouring of this representation, like all the symbolism of the Apocalypse, is derived from the Old Testament, and carries us back to many a sweet ancient word of psalmist and prophet. Especially is there an allusion in the former of these passages to the words of Isa. xlix. 10, and it is noteworthy that the same office which the earlier words ascribed to God is here unhesitatingly attributed in even higher form to the Lamb.

There is a striking anomaly, and at first sight incongruity, in that daring symbol, that the Lamb is the Shepherd. But the reality underlying the symbol is that Jesus Christ, by His death, becomes the Guide, Protector, and Nourisher of men. We may perhaps venture still further to draw from the incongruity of the symbol the great truth that the Leader of men is one in nature with the men whom He leads. The Shepherd is Himself a Lamb, and is our Leader just because He shares our nature. But that is not in the intention of the seer, and can only be taken as a permissible play of allusion on our parts.

We are on firmer ground when we see in this sweet metaphor the thought that the Christ who died and reigns is the eternal Pattern for us, whether on earth or in the calm perfection of Mount Zion. Here we have to go after the Shepherd and Overseer of our souls, who has left us an example that we should tread in His steps. Here we follow afar off, lingering, straying, and all unfit to tread in

His footprints. There "they shall follow the Lamb whithersoever He goeth," with complete imitation, and steps not unequal to His. But for both states, to follow Him is blessedness and to be like Him is perfection. Nor shall that future be without advance. There will be growing approximation to Him, a more perfect conformity to His likeness, a fuller appropriation of His life, and an ever-increasing nearness to Him which shall fill eternity with freshness, and make its joys and service ever new.

The symbol suggests that the slain and enthroned Lamb is, by both characteristics, the Source of security and the Author of nourishment. True, there will be no outward dangers to guard against; but the reason why "they shall hunger no more, neither thirst any more, neither shall the sun strike upon them, nor any heat," is, "for the Lamb which is in the midst of the throne shall be their Shepherd," and therefore are they safe from evil, and replenished with all good. He is the eternal Source of satisfaction for heaven as for earth, and is Himself the Fountain of living waters to which He leads the flock. Heaven is Christ, and Christ is Heaven. The future state of the redeemed is stable blessedness and full delight, not because of physical changes or added glories, but because Christ is theirs, and the full issues of His cross and reign are reaped by them in their following the Shepherd-Lamb, and sharing with Him His glories.

The relation of the flock to the shepherd in the good pastures of the mountains of Israel above is in some respects the opposite of that experienced here, and in others the completion of it. There we shall have no valley of the shadow of death, no ravenous beasts to prowl round the fold and pounce upon the wanderers from the flock, no dark gorges, no stony ways, no thirsty deserts, no straying in the wilderness and tearing the fleeces among thorns, no losing sight of the Shepherd, and panting with panic fears. There the Shepherd needs no weapons—neither rod to smite nor sling to defend. If we give ourselves to His gentle guidance here, where all these terrors and hindrances are, He will bring us thither where they are not; and if, with stumbling steps, we try to follow Him as we best can in this rough road, He will seek us when we wander, and restore us when we faint, and bring us to the one fold, where we shall be near Him, and at rest for evermore. But there is a grim verse in one of the psalms which tells us of another shepherd whose flock consists of those self-destroying souls, who will not take the Lamb for their Sacrifice, King, and Guide. Of these we read, "Death shall be their shepherd," and the fold to which they are driven is the shambles. The choice is before us. Shall we be of the flock of the good Shepherd, or of that which is marked for the slaughter?

IV. The final group of passages to which we direct attention represents Jesus as the Warrior-Lamb.

"These shall war against the Lamb, and the Lamb shall overcome them; for He is Lord of lords, and King of kings." So is the conflict between the vassal kings of the beast and the conquering Christ described in one vision of this book, while in that portraying the final conflict, though the name with which we are here concerned is not employed, the same title is given to the victor, which in the passage just quoted is ascribed to the Lamb. "He hath on His vesture and on His thigh a name written, King of kings, and Lord of lords."

The very strangeness and incongruity of the combination of the ideas of the Lamb and of warfare is part of the felicity of the symbol. For so is the thought set forth that Christ conquers by gentleness, and that the instrument by which He subdues is the great manifestation of His love in His sacrifice. But, further, the paradox of the Warrior-Lamb hints at the terrible possibilities of destructive wrath which lie as dormant in that gentle Christ. The same double aspect of His character and energy is set forth in the striking juxtaposition in the context of our second text: "Behold, the Lion of the tribe of Judah . . . and I beheld, and, lo, a Lamb." Nothing is so terrible as the wrath of gentle love and patience. No wonder that the rebels against the long-suffering, meek Christ, when they see Him coming in the clouds of heaven, call despairingly on rocks and hills to crush them, if thereby they may be hid from the "wrath of the Lamb." Divine love is not incapable of anger. The Lamb of God is the Lion of Judah. Let us not trifle with His power to smite and rend. The Lion of the tribe of Judah is the Lamb of God. Let us trust and take refuge in His power to heal and save.

But this vision of the conquering gentleness, which overcomes by sacrifice, derives still further significance when contrasted with its antagonist. The Lamb and the Beast are the two powers arrayed against each other. Now, it is profitless to ask whether there has been or will be a personal manifestation of the tendencies which are embodied in that image. It is more to the purpose to inquire, What makes the beast a beast, whoever or wherever he may be? And the answer is not far to seek. What did God mean manhood to be? Is not union with Him, in love, desire, and obedience, the ideal for man; and does not the humanity which is separated from him and self-centred, sink to the animal level, and become like, and therein beneath, the beasts that know not the Divine hand that feeds them, and can have no other object than themselves in their dumb and narrow lives? The God-centred man is truly a man; the self-centred man is somewhat less than a man. Where these self-regarding impulses are supreme the animalizing process is complete, and "the beast" is the perfection of that imperfection—the embodiment, as it were, of self separated from God. Against that sinful selfhood Jesus fights now, and He will help us, if we will, in our daily struggle with the beast in our own natures. If we will open our hearts to the cleansing of His sacrifice, the authority of His reign, the guidance of His Shepherd's care, He will fill them with power which shall make us victorious over all in ourselves that draws us away from God, and "the lion and the dragon" that are in us we "shall trample underfoot."

The Warrior-Lamb is the Hope of each soul struggling with its own evil and seeking to help its fellows. He is the Hope for the world. They who understand the meaning of His sacrifice, enthronement, gracious guidance, and protection, cannot but be confident that He will cast out evil, and that the fruit of the travail of His soul shall be rich and ample and eternal enough to satisfy even the universal love of His heart, and to correspond to even the might of His sacrifice and the unspeakable price with which He has redeemed the world.

For ourselves, all depends on our beginning with the vision of the slain Lamb. The call comes to each of us, "Behold the Lamb of God, that taketh away the sin of the world!" Our sins are in that gigantic mass beneath which He sank fainting, but which He has borne away. Have we laid our hands, like the offerers of old, on the head of the sacrifice and thus associated ourselves with Him by faith?

Have we ever truly cried, "O Lamb of God, that taketh away the sins of the world, have mercy upon us"? If we truly and habitually live obeying the merciful call to behold Him, then in life He will be for us Sacrifice, King, Shepherd, Champion. If we look to Him through the mists and clouds of time, His face will beam upon us and make the darkness light about us. When He leads us through the valley of the shadow of death and the swellings of Jordan, He will be with us; and when we open our eyes again, after the brief darkness, and wipe the cold waters from our faces, our first sight in heaven will be the Lamb in the midst of the throne, and He will lead us among the good pastures of the sunlit hills, where no foes nor fears will disturb, nor sin and sorrow vex any more for ever.

SPOKEN NEED, UNSPOKEN REQUEST.

SPOKEN NEED, UNSPOKEN REQUEST.

"And when they wanted wine, the mother of Jesus saith unto Him, They have no wine."—JOHN ii. 3.

"Therefore his sisters sent unto Jesus, saying, Lord, behold, he whom Thou lovest is sick."—JOHN xi. 3.

THERE can be no greater contrast than that presented by these two scenes. In the one we have the homely merriment of a rustic wedding, in the other the despair of two desolate women's hearts. The mother of Jesus and the sisters of Lazarus stand at opposite poles of feeling. But from the station of each a straight line can be drawn to where Jesus is. Sorrow and joy have an equally open road to Him, and find equal sympathy there. The gravity of the respective needs in these two incidents is singularly different. The one is a trifle, the other a crushing weight. But, great or small, transient or lifelong, as cares or wants may be, they are best met and conquered and supplied when told to our Lord. Not less noticeable is the identity in manner of the two sayings. The mother of our Lord simply says, "They have no wine," and adds no more. The sisters send only the message, "He whom Thou lovest is sick," and proffer no request. That manner of addressing Christ, alike in sorrow and joy, in trivial and in great necessity, with the simple statement of what presses on life or heart, and the suppression of all prescription to Him of what He is to do, may suggest some not useless considerations as to the tone and manner which should mark our intercourse with Jesus.

I. Our intercourse with Him should be characterized by frank familiarity of communication, such as befits love and friendship.

It was a natural impulse which brought both these utterances to Jesus. His mother was troubled when the scanty store of her friends at Cana began to give out, and, as she saw the wine-skins becoming more and more flaccid, a spirit in her feet carried her to her Son, perhaps before she well knew what she did, or wished Him to do. The two sad hearts at Bethany, as they saw the black wing of the angel of death hovering over their home, turned spontaneously to Jesus, and, though they did not know what He could do if He came, still felt that the sorrow would be more easily borne if they knew that He knew it. Now, that same instinctive prompting to tell dear ones all our thoughts and wishes is an unfailing character of real love. It makes the blessedness of many a happy pair of hearts, to whom knowing and being known are equal delight and simple necessity. The depth and purity of our human love may be roughly, but with tolerable accuracy, measured by the strength of that impulse. Where reserve is possible, love is shallow or coarse. The impulse affects all that interests or concerns a pair of friends. Not even dark secrets of shame escape, for true love seeks to share these too, and they are less of a barrier when told than when hidden. The magnitude of the thing is of no importance. We do not ask whether it is large enough to trouble those whom we love with it. A child runs to its mother with a broken toy, or the scratch of a pin on its finger, or an untied shoe. Love has no care for great or small. Concealment of little is concealment also of much, and the confidence which tells trifles is perhaps greater than that which tells important things; and what love prizes is the confidence, more than the knowledge given.

The love which binds human hearts to one another is not different in kind from that which knits men to Jesus. Love is love, to whomsoever it is directed and whatever may be the differences of its accompaniments. What our love does in us when it is fixed on one another, that it should do when it is fixed in humble faith on Jesus Christ. Many of its signs and effects will necessarily be different, but in the one case, as in the other, perfect frankness of communication and delight in yielding to the impulse of laying bare every corner of our hearts, whatever inner baseness may lurk there, will assuredly attend real love. We may live in the light of an ever-gladdening consciousness of Christ's love and sympathy, and if we walked in that light as we may, and therefore should, we should no more be able to carry secret cares hidden beneath our cloaks to gnaw at our hearts, than loving husband or wife can hide troubles or thoughts from wife or husband loved.

Now, that is a very sharp test of Christian character, and makes short work of much complacent profession. If we really love Christ and feel to Him as to a friend, and if we heartily believe that we can speak to Him and be heard, we shall not need any one to tell us that it is our duty to pray to Him. "Access with confidence" will come spontaneously, as a relief to overcharged hearts and the blessing of solitary ones—and, after all companionship, who is not solitary? The impossibility of imparting our whole selves to any makes our hearts often ache, and if we feel to Christ as we should, we shall thankfully still the aching by uttermost frankness of self-revelation to Him. We should instinctively feel that whatever irritates or affects us, be it slight as a mosquito's puncture or grave as a whip-adder's sting, must be told to Him. He who only invokes Christ's sympathy and help when there comes a "knot" in his fortunes which he thinks "worthy" of such a hand to unravel, will seldom invoke Him, and will not usually do it to much purpose. Trifles are the bulk of life, and unless our communion with our Lord extends to trifles, it will be poor and partial indeed. We may well ask ourselves, then, whether such instinctive impulse, prior to all reflection as to duty or advantage, sends us to Jesus Christ, to make Him our confidant and unload our hearts to Him, in that frank outpouring which is the native tongue of love. Do we find ourselves telling Him of our annoyances, calamities, little wants and the like, almost before we know it? There are heights and depths of Christian communion beyond such self-regarding speech, but these sanctities and sublimities will seldom be reached except we first have acquired the habit of telling Him all that interests and harasses us in daily life. The mountain summits of a continent do not usually rise at the water's edge, but from high uplands. How different our lives would be if we brought them all in their veriest trifles into touch with Jesus—noble, calm, joyous in the midst of sorrow, and with a certain breath of heaven rustling through them and freshening them! "Pour out your hearts before Him," as a man might invert some golden vase, and empty its contents to the last drop trickling from the lip. The heart thus emptied in frank confidence will be filled with peace, and be conscious of an all-sufficing presence.

II. These two sayings may further suggest the trustful and submissive suppression of desire which should accompany this frank confidence.

"They have no wine." Did that mean, "Give them some"? It can scarcely be supposed that, at that early stage, the virgin expected her Son to work a miracle, even though she kept all the unforgetable events of the Nativity in her heart. "He whom Thou lovest is sick." Did that mean, "Come and heal him"? Some faint hope of that sort may have been in the sisters' hearts, as may be inferred from their half-reproachful greeting of Jesus when He came, but it was probably of the vaguest character. If there were such wishes in either case, the suppression of them indicates the speakers' absolute trust in Christ's superior wisdom and perfect sympathy, which makes their utterance of their wishes superfluous and presumptuous. But probably in neither case was there a definite expectation, and if there were anything in their minds beyond the impulse of which we have spoken, they apparently trustfully left the decision of what He should do in His own hands.

Let us tell Christ our needs and stop there. Surely we are well enough acquainted with His loving purpose to be certain that for Him to know is to pity, and to pity is to stretch out a full and strong hand of supply and help. We say that we believe in His Divine nature. If we do, we must believe that His knowledge needs no informing by us to move His sympathy. Why, then, should we tell Him our needs, if He knows them already? We have already partly answered that question by pointing to the instinct of love; but, further, we must remember that our communication of our wants is preliminary to His supply of them, not because it informs Him, but because it prepares us. He does not need to be told, but we need to tell Him. That being so, it is the part of faith to spread our needs before Jesus, and to do no more. All need makes appeal to Him, and many forms of it are supplied from His loving hand, without other prayer than the dumb, unconscious one of the necessity's existence. "He heareth the ravens when they cry; He openeth His hand, and satisfieth the desire of every living thing." When on earth, many miracles were wrought without either faith or petition. "He healed them that had need of healing," for no other reason than because they had need, and the silent pleading of their misery entered into His heart. That rock needed no stroke of a rod, nor even a word, to make its waters gush forth. The presence of the thirsty was enough.

But for higher gifts there must needs be the confidence already spoken of, and where that exists there need not and should not be the prescribing of a course to Jesus. To do that is consonant neither with faith nor with reverence. Humble submission to Christ's better wisdom breathed through His mother's words and the sisters' message. True prayer is not pestering the Throne with passionate entreaties that a certain method of deliverance, which seems best to us, should be forthwith effected, but is a calm utterance of need, and a patient, submissive expectance of fitting help, of which we dare not define the manner or the time. They are wisest, most trustful and reverent, who do not seek to impose their notions and wills on the clearer wisdom and deeper love to which they betake themselves, but are satisfied with leaving all to His arbitrament. True prayer is the bending of our own wills to the Divine, not the urging of ours on it. When Hezekiah received the insolent letter from the invader, he took it and "spread it before the

Lord," asking God to read it, and leaving all else to Him to determine; as if he had said, "Behold, Lord, this boasting page. I bring it to Thee, and now it is Thine affair more than mine." The burden which we roll on God lies lightly on our shoulders; and if we do roll it thither, we need not trouble ourselves with the question of how He will deal with it.

The less we seek to prescribe to God, the truer and more blessed will be our intercourse with Him. It is enough to tell Him that the wine fails, or that Lazarus is ill. Leave Him a free hand to do as He will, in supplying deficiencies and healing diseases. A confident assurance of the fact that needs will be met, a blank sheet in our expectation as to how they will be, and a sharpened attention, alert to mark the direction which His help may take, should ever accompany our speech to Christ. The highest prayer is, "Not my will, but Thine, be done," and the best answer is, "The peace of God shall keep your hearts and minds in Christ Jesus." The cares which are imparted to the beloved lose their poison, the tasks shared with them are lightened, and all joys become more joyful, and all objects of interest more poignantly stimulating when shared. The law of earthly love applies to the highest, in so far that to tell Jesus of burdens shifts them from us to Him, and disturbances are less disturbing when our disquiet has been breathed into His calm heart. Mary shook off responsibility for the empty wine-skins when she told Jesus of them, and we bring a stronger arm than ours to deal with difficulties when we in like manner speak of them to our Lord. The sisters at Bethany felt less lonely and crushed when they thought that Jesus knew, though they did not venture to send requests to Him. So from these two instances, the one of a most trivial need, the other of a most tragic, we may learn the one lesson—tell your need, and then be silent, and let Him settle how it is to be met. Only be on the watch for what He may do, and be sure that He will do something, and that the right thing.

III. These two incidents give two ways of taking Christ's delays.

Our Lord's treatment of the two appeals is substantially the same. The answer to Mary sounds more repellent in English than in Greek, inasmuch as "woman" has in it a tinge of roughness not conveyed by the original. The question simply suggests independent action and not alienation; but the request was certainly put aside, and its repetition forbidden. In the remaining clause, "Mine hour is not yet come," a promise, like a sweet kernel, is hidden in the words; for "not yet" warrants and seems to be meant to create expectance that the hour will strike soon, and be heard by His ear. Precisely similar is Christ's action in the other case. "When Jesus heard that he was sick, He abode still two days in the same place where He was." There again he delayed till His "hour" had come. That expression, so frequent on our Lord's lips, implies that each act of His was regulated by the conviction, clear to Himself, that the time for it, appointed by the Father, had arrived. Whether it were the hour "when the Son of man should be glorified" by the supreme sacrifice of the cross, or the hour when the peasant wedding should have replenished stores, His ear heard it strike, without the possibility of mistake; and till it was heard, nothing—not even a mother's wistful look, or the sad hearts at Bethany—could induce Him to act. In proportion as we approach the same perfection of filial obedience, we shall be blessed with the same certainty of perception, and may hear, even amid the vulgar, loud noises of life, the solemn tones announcing the hour for great service or small duty. Well for those who have so silenced the ringing in their own ears that they hear beyond mistake God's chimes, and hearing, obey!

The time between Christ's refusal to act on His mother's hint and His acting on it was probably brief; but much may happen in short space, and requisite conditions may have been quickly supplied. God's clock does not go at the same rate as ours, but "a thousand years" may sometimes be crowded into "one" of His days, and one of His days be lengthened to a slow thousand of our years. Two days seemed an eternity to the sisters, and no doubt bewilderingly long to some of the attendant disciples; but, longer or shorter, the delays teach us the truth that Christ's time is determined by considerations which we are little able to appreciate. "The Lord is not slack concerning His promises, as men count slackness." The same connection of ideas is presented also in that remarkable incident which this evangelist alone records, when our Lord's brethren scoffingly suggested to Him to go up to the feast, and received the same answer as did Mary, "My time is not yet come." It came in a few hours, and probably was marked to Christ's consciousness by an inward impulse rather than by any change in circumstances. Thus, an action which looked like mere vacillation, and has often been felt as a difficulty, becomes, when rightly understood, a striking witness to the continual communion with the guiding will of the Father, and regulation of all His life thereby, which Jesus enjoyed and practised. But, in regard to His answers to our requests, as in regard to His answers to those in our texts, though the considerations which determine His hour are beyond our sight, the great governing principle of which they were products is clear. Whatever holds back His hand, it is not lack of sympathy with our sorrow, disregard of our confidence, nor unwillingness nor inability to respond to our cry. The consideration of what is best for us and others who may be helped by our experience is sovereign with Him. All delay is the result of His love, and meant for highest good, not only to the individual most concerned, but to others also. "I am glad for your sakes that I was not there, to the intent ye may believe."

The similarity which we have traced in the two superficially so different instances does not extend to the manner in which the two delays were received by the persons interested. These are contrasted rather than parallel, and while the one is an example, the other is a warning. Mary's meek faith, though there had been so little hitherto to feed it, drew hope from the seeming rebuff. Apparently she clung to the glimmer of hope in that "not yet," else her charge to the servants has nothing in the narrative to account for it. It was but a slight foothold, but it was enough for her. A heart truly in harmony with Christ will ever hear in His most discouraging words the undertones of promise. "Not yet" may darken to-day, but it ensures a bright to-morrow. "If winter comes, can spring be far behind?" The very sorrow is a veiled prophet, and the night of weeping leads in the morning of joy. That was a noble and wise faith which bore away from Christ's "not yet," not fear, doubt, disappointment, nor the sense of repulse, but a hope certain as to the fact of His help, and quietly ignorant of the time and way. "Whatsoever He saith unto you, do it," was a triumph of faith, penetrating the surface denial, and sucking the sweet drop stored in the depths of the flower. The six waterpots full of wine vindicated the confidence which translated "not yet" into "in good time." So will it be with us, if we leave Him to settle when "right early" is. We shall "wonder at the beauteous hours, the slow result of winter showers," and see at last what we believed while He tarried, that delay is a form of love, and His hour the right hour.

The two sisters at Bethany seem to have had natural regrets during the four days between their message and Christ's coming. Apparently, indeed, their brother was already dead when their messenger reached our Lord. But, if we may judge from the salutation with which each met Him, " If Thou hadst been here, my brother had not died," they had often wearily looked at one another in their lonely misery and said the same thing. How we may recognize ourselves in them! That same weakening and useless regret that something did not happen which, if it had happened, would have changed everything, tortures us all in our sorrows. The sisters did not so much complain as regret. They did not think that Jesus should or might have come, they only thought—How blessed if He had come, or never gone! They had to learn the purpose of His delay and of their sorrow, and when in a few minutes they did learn it, how ashamed of their "if" they must have been! The delay to heal was in order to prepare a mightier blessing, and the sharp sorrow was allowed in order that its wounds might be filled with fragrant balm, which only a wounded heart could receive. It was more to give back to empty hands the blessing that had been torn from them than to have kept it there. Jesus did not come to heal the brother who was sick, because He would come to restore to the sisters' embrace the brother that "was dead and is alive again, was lost" in the dark grave, "and found again" in the gladsome light of life.

So it ever is with the experience of those who wait His time, nor let their faith droop, nor doubt that His absence and their sorrows are the fruits of His love and the preparation for larger blessings and deeper joy. So He vindicates His delays. So He answers the confidence which tells Him all its needs and troubles, and leaves Him to determine how and when to work. So He rewards the faithful and submissive prayer, of which the inmost spirit is, "Not my will, but Thine; not my time, but Thine!'

GLIMPSES OF THE HEART OF JESUS.

D—2

GLIMPSES OF THE HEART OF JESUS.

"Being moved with compassion, He stretched forth His hand."—
MARK i. 41.

THE Gospels seldom speak of what Jesus felt. They are for the most part content to let His words and deeds speak for themselves, as they have indeed spoken, leaving an impression, marvellous in its clearness, depth, and universality, when compared with the four tiny booklets which have made it.

But this evangelist somewhat more frequently than the others lifts a corner of the veil, and gives a momentary glimpse into the holy of holies in the heart of Jesus. If the old idea that Peter was the source of this Gospel is true, we have a natural explanation of its minute details, and can picture the apostle, whose quickness of observation was accelerated and sharpened by passionate love, watching with keen eye, and remembering in a faithful memory, every look and gesture and fleeting expression of countenance which told of the heart's emotions. The image of Christ enshrined in the hearts of men owes much of its sweetness to the small traits contributed by this evangelist to the common stock. We purpose, then, in this sermon, to deal with Mark's glimpses of the heart of Jesus, of which the words taken as our text are the earliest.

It may be well at the outset to enumerate them. There is first the compassion noted in the text. Next we have (ch. iii. 5) anger blended with grief at the hardening of His opponents' hearts. Further, we find two instances in ch. vi.: one (ver. 6), wonder at unbelief; and another (ver. 34), compassion for the helplessness of the untaught multitude. There are also two instances in ch. x., in which are recorded our Lord's displeasure with the disciples' keeping children from His embrace, and the outgoing of His love to the young ruler. Then there is a solemn and pathetic pair in ch. xiv.: one, the evangelist's description of Jesus as "sore amazed and very heavy;" and the other, His own plaintive word to the three drowsy disciples: "My soul is exceeding sorrowful, even unto death." If we study the picture resulting from the combination of all these, we may gain some deepened impressions of the glory and sweetness of that pure manhood, which may knit our thankful hearts in closer affection and service to Him.

I. We note then, first, the Christ who pities all sorrow.

The two instances in which compassion is attributed to our Lord by Mark may be taken as covering the whole ground of human misery. The former is that in our text, which represents the pity that welled forth at the sight of physical suffering. The other (ch. vi. 34) is that in which the emotion sprang up at the sight of the weary multitude who had followed Him for His teaching, as His penetrating gaze looked beneath their bodily weariness to their spiritual want of guidance from prophet, priest, or ruler. Thus, physical evil and spiritual darkness and weariness smote on His heart. Once besides in this Gospel we find Christ's compassion mentioned, but by Himself, not by the evangelist (ch. viii. 6), when He assigns it as His motive for consulting the disciples as to how the crowds are to be fed. Luke, who only once speaks of our Lord's compassion, does so in connection with a specially sad story, that of the poor woman whom Jesus and His disciples met as they toiled up the hill to Nain, weeping behind the bier of the sole light of her widowed home, her only son. No wonder that such grief and such loneliness touched the springs of pity in His solitary heart. Matthew, too, tells of our Lord's compassion in the parallel passage to our text, and in other places.

These two cases teach us the impartial width of our Lord's compassion. He was open to appeals to His pity made by sickness, hunger, and the other ills that flesh is heir to, and He was not less quickly and deeply touched by compassion for ignorance, spiritual and intellectual want of guidance, and the weariness and unrest which these caused. Such capacity of feeling with equal strength the appeal of the two great forms of man's misery is rare, and more frequently we find that the men who are quick to pity the hungry and the sick have little sympathy for the ignorant and them that are out of the way, while, on the other hand, the compassion of religious men is often apt to be somewhat indifferent to material wants, and to leave dealing with them to others. So it comes to pass that there are two sets of philanthropists in the world, who do not look at each other with altogether friendly eyes, the one of whom cares for men's bodies, and thinks it rather waste to spend pity and effort on their "souls," and the other of whom is so much concerned about their souls that it gives little help to attempts to improve material conditions.

The Church has often laid itself open to the world's taunt of neglecting the lower needs, which are more clamorous than the higher; but there are many tokens that a clearer understanding of the width of Christian compassion and duty is beginning to prevail. Possibly the warning against the impending possibility of harmful exaggeration in a new direction may not be unnecessary. The new impulses to recognizing the mission of Christianity in regard to social questions are sure to carry some light weights too far. As Luther says somewhere, in his rough strong way, "Human nature is like a drunken peasant. If he is put up on one side of his horse, he is sure to fall over on the other." It will be a dark day for the progress of the Christian Church if good men suffer themselves to be drawn aside from its primary work, the preaching of the gospel and the dealing with the deepest sources of human misery in human sin, to throwing their chief energy into the needful but secondary work of dealing with the fruits of spiritual evil in physical distress. It is true that Jesus pitied the hungry and fed them, and therein He has taught us how wide our sympathies and efforts should be, but it is also true that He rebuked the crowds who came after Him only for loaves, and pressed upon them as His true and proper gift the flesh and blood which are the sources and supports of a better life.

Christ's sympathy was incalculably deeper and more poignant than ours can ever be. For His eye was clearer than ours, and saw deeper. To Him the single sufferer represented crowds. The one black drop brought to His mind all the sullen ocean of blackness, which rolls its heavy tides round the whole world. We see but the wave or two that break nearest us, and all the other multitudinous billows escape our knowledge. We mass men in the race, and, generalizing, lose the impression of individuals. We have a vague notion that there is a great deal of sorrow in the world, but we do not receive the impact of it all on our own hearts as Jesus Christ did. He saw as a God what he pitied as a Man. His compassion was not only the pity of a Divine nature which, if it be love, must needs be pity too, but it was the fellow-feeling of one of ourselves, which knew a kindred pang, and was fed by a Divine clearness and sweep of perception that summoned up before Him on the occasion of one bier all the mourners and the dead, and saw in every sorrow but the nearest member of a linked procession girdling the world. Nor did the underlying Divine knowledge alone deepen His sympathy. The purity of His manhood increased it. In Him were no spots insensitive by reason of selfishness, as there are in all others—true witches' marks, which can be pricked without feeling. A soul entirely delivered from selfish regards would be like an infant's hand for sensitiveness, whereas our palms are indurated in the cuticle by selfishness, and our fingers have lost the fineness of touch which would secure sympathy with others' sorrows. With Jesus it was as if the very nerves of His own frame had been prolonged into that of others, so close was His union with them, by the wonderful completeness of his self-oblivion. Thus in truest fashion His sympathy answered to the meaning of the word, which so far transcends the ordinary manifestations of it in our hearts, being a real suffering together with those whom He pitied. Our selfishness puts an armour of brass over our hearts, through which the sharp point of others' woes scarcely reaches us, except as a dull blow that does not pierce deeply enough to bring the blood; but Jesus came among men with His naked breast exposed to all the slings and arrows that were showered on all, and He was sore wounded by them all. His pity was His life. He was a Man of sorrows because He bare our griefs and carried our sorrows, and the burden was laid upon His shoulders by the perfectness of His pity which made them all His own, long before He fainted beneath the cross on the short journey from the judgment-hall to Calvary. Christ's pity was essential to His service of men. "Looking up to heaven, He sighed, and said, Ephphatha." The sigh had to come before the word of power could come. He was not only impelled to put forth His miraculous power by the cries of the sufferers or of their intercessors, but sometimes by the quick spontaneous outgoing of His own pity. Before men called He answered, for His own heart anticipated their desires. His pity was no luxurious idle emotion, but the impulse to action. The like should be true of all Christians. No help can be rightly rendered unless it come from a sympathetic heart. Much Christian work is spoiled and made worse than useless by being done in hard, supercilious fashion. Benefits need to be wrapped in softest down of sympathy, or they will cut the hand that receives them. A man may be knocked down by a charitable gift flung at his head like a stone. For all forms of Christian service the law is valid—without sympathy no good will be done. Nor is the converse less needful to remember—that without practical issues no sympathy is worth anything. Not merely is it useless to benefit the sufferers, but it harms the person cherishing it. Every emotion which is allowed to rise and pass without its appropriate action tends to harden the heart. If mercy is twice blessed, lazy compassion is twice cursed.

Christ's sympathy clings to Him still, and is a permanent attribute of His perpetual and exalted manhood. He bears our griefs on His heart now, and bends over us each with as true a knowledge of our trouble, and as complete a partaking of it, as when on earth He wept by the grave of Lazarus, or felt the loneliness of that sonless widow. If our griefs be small and affecting mainly our material fortunes, we may take heart to believe that since they are great enough to trouble us they are not too small to move His sympathy, when we remember that He Himself declared that He "had compassion on the multitude" because they were hungry.

II. We note the Christ who feels anger, grief, and wonder because of men's evil.

We find one instance in ch. iii. 5, in which He "looked on them with anger, being grieved at the hardening of their heart." The word rendered "grieved" is a compound term expressing the coexistence of some other feeling with the anger. Again we find (ch. x. 14) that our Lord was "moved with indignation" (R.V.). In the first case, the cause of the anger was the obstinate and increasing obduracy of the Pharisees, who had no eyes for anything but a breach of ceremonial law, into which they hoped He would be led. All the beauty of His character, all the power of His words, the mystery of His miraculous working, the joy of the cured man, were nothing to them. That the cure was a miracle brought no conviction to their minds, which could only grasp the fact that the miracle was a breach of rabbinical law. In the second case, the disciples, as it were, dammed up the flow of His tenderness and interfered with access to His mercy. So the evils which especially drew forth His anger were not the gross flagrant transgressions of notorious evil livers, but the sins of formal religionists to whom sacrifice was more than mercy, and of disciples who had imperfectly apprehended the continual flow and width of His love. Surely the lesson is needed at all times and in all Churches. Nothing more effectually blinds to the highest vision of Jesus Christ than a pedantic overestimate of the mere externals of religion. How many of us would not listen to a prophet or to Christ Himself, if He neglected or brushed aside our jealously guarded ceremonials and proprieties of worship! On the other hand, how often Christian Churches and individuals have, like the disciples, put hindrances in the way of the "little ones" coming to Him! How often have misplaced regard for the honour of the Master, and other even less reputable motives, forbidden humble souls to draw near for His embracing arm and the benediction of His lips! A sharper accent marks Christ's rebuke to His disciples, who cluster round Him like a bodyguard to keep off the profane, lest they should by their continual coming weary Him, than that which remonstrated with far more coarse guilt.

But that anger was not all which these sins excited in His heart. Through the thunder-cloud looked the sun, and across the heavy drops was flung the rainbow. Grief blended with Christ's anger. Both emotions must be in that perfect manhood, which is at once the realization of the human ideal and the revelation of the Divine reality. Their union saves us from the misconception of His anger. There can be no heat of passion in it, for it burns side by side with a great fountain of sorrowing pity which would quench any such blaze of wrath. His anger is a noble Divine aversion from evil. Unless Jesus is but half a man and maimed of an essential element in healthy and wholesouled humanity, there must be in Him a true recognition of the badness of bad things and an indignant recoil from these. Nor is such aversion less inseparable from lofty conceptions of the Divine nature than from true ones of the human. Nor is there any malevolence in Christ's anger. It is but a low kind of anger which includes the desire for evil on its objects. The highest kind necessarily includes the opposite desire, as every parent and child knows. Evil-doers are to be blamed but pitied too, and however rigorously retribution may be awarded to them, compassion is not to be withheld. Jesus saw the essential character of sin as none else can do, and He knew its issue. Therefore He "grieved" and "was angry," in a blended stream of emotion wherein the darker current neighboured without weakening the other, which in turn accompanied and softened without diluting its sister-flow.

That union of anger and grief saves us from exaggeration of His pity, as if He could not condemn or punish. His compassion does not contradict, nor put in the background, the certainty of His righteous judgment. The two are perfectly harmonious. The tears that fell for Jerusalem did not hinder Him from pronouncing her doom, nor did the judicial act of sentencing arrest the tears. Many modern representations of the gentle Christ need correction, for what they call gentleness is nothing nobler than weakness. Let us not forget that the Lamb of God is the Lion of Judah, and that even the Lamb "has seven horns." All ruth and pity are in Him, but in Him, too, are righteous anger and fiery indignation. The revelations of an earlier time are not cancelled. God in Christ is still "a consuming fire," but in Him we learn that side by side with that fire, or perhaps we may even say, as a necessary element in it, burns lambent the white flame of infinite tenderness and pity. In their deepest roots wrath and pity are one, even as the heat which blisters and the light which gladdens have the same source.

But there is another glimpse given us by Mark of the manner in which men's evils affected Jesus, in that remarkable expression that He "marvelled at their unbelief" (ch. vi. 6). We are apt to wonder that Christ could wonder, seeing that He knew what was in man. But His manhood was under distinct limitations in regard to knowledge, and the fact that He shared that feeling too is precious, as attesting how truly He emptied Himself of His glory when He assumed the fashion of a man. In another place we read that He also wondered with happier wonder at the ripe faith of a heathen. Here He marvels at the dogged unbelief of "His own." If unbelief evoked Christ's astonishment, how unreasonable and contrary to all probability it must be! It may have an "excuse," or rather those guilty of it may "make excuses" for it; but these are only got up for show, and are not its real reason, which is found in that perfection of unreason which prefers death to life. The mystery of the world is sin. If we could explain it, we should know all things. It can give no rational account of itself. Try to put the reasons for it into plain words, and their blank irrationality is manifest. What reason can there be why men should be blind to facts which stare them in the face, and should deliberately choose ruin, and turn away from their highest good, and, admitting the most tremendous truths, should straightway proceed to huddle them out of sight lest they should influence conduct? All sin is flagrant unreason, and nothing is more marvellous than that the beauty and sweetness of Jesus should be resisted, and His offered gifts refused.

His meek heart had been well schooled in the possibilities of men's unkindness and contempt; but, even in its calm, a moment of wonder rose when once again He was forced to feel that He called in vain, and in vain loved. Thus His whole soul was disturbed by contact with sin. It left Him grieved and hurt, wounded and saddened. The compulsory association of some pure heart with criminals and profligates, as in some prison where an innocent man is shut up with criminals, and "vexed" in soul with their "filthy conversation," is but a faint shadow of what Christ bore all His life long. He was "a Man of sorrows, and acquainted with grief," because He "dwelt among them that are set on fire," and all this sorrow, pity, and wonder He bore because He loved the men who thus tortured Him, even as He loves us who can still grieve Him, and may still find balm in His compassion.

III. We note, further, the Christ yearning in love towards very imperfect desires after good.

Mark tells us that Jesus "looking upon" the young ruler "loved him." There was much about the youth to draw out love. He was ingenuous, earnest in his desire to do right, had restrained his passions in his hot early manhood, and aspired with some genuine lifting of desire after the world to come. But there were flaws in his character which Jesus manifestly read from the beginning of the conversation. He had but a superficial notion of goodness, and a false conception of the requisites for inheriting eternal life. To him "good" was a thing to "do," and " eternal life" was wholly future, and was payment for acts done here, not because he loved them, but because he wanted their wages. He had so little apprehension of the sweep of the Divine Law, that he was certain that his obedience had been comprehensive of all its precepts and unbroken through his life. And when the final test was put he failed, and thereby proved that there was something in him deeper than the desire for goodness or for eternal life. Yet, for all the flaws, Jesus loved him, and would fain have drawn wholly to Himself a character with so many buds of promise in it.

The great heart of Jesus Christ has room in it for all evil-doers, and bends with pitying sorrow over debased wills that cleave to earth, and paralyzed spirits that have no touch of aspiration after things lovely and of good report. His love rests with peculiar tenderness on those who have yielded themselves wholly to Him and are walking in the light with Him. But there is a third class, touched with yearning after something higher than they possess, and yet not brought to the point of following Jesus with clear resolve and entire surrender; and on these, too, His love falls. A harsh word, like a hasty blow struck at a feeble fire, may put out a spark which care would have fostered; but Jesus does not "quench the dimly burning wick," nor frown away imperfect seekers after a better life. What would become of any of us, if He was not patient with partial knowledge and superficial conceptions of good? It befits His followers to cherish the beginnings and faint dawnings of such in others, as their Lord did, and as they themselves need that He should do with them. For the most advanced and perfect saint on earth is nearer the most incomplete beginner who has but turned his face to the far-off light, than he is to the light to which both are looking and neither have attained. Degrees of imperfection should not despise one another. One arc of a circle may be swept through more degrees of circumference than another, but it is only an unfinished arc after all.

Christ's love for imperfect goodness is shown in His clear laying down of the stringent conditions with which it must comply in order to be complete. It was precisely because Jesus, looking on His youthful and eager questioner, "loved him," that "He said unto him, One thing thou lackest," and demanded of him the surrender of all that he had, and the following of Him. Frankness is the truest kindness. What such characters as the ruler's most need is to see clearly that aspirations and outward acts are not enough, and that it is no slight matter to be "good," but one demanding the entire suppression of self and the use of all possessions as auxiliary thereto. He had been playing with wishes and surface virtues long enough. If he were in earnest, he would welcome the call which showed him the depths. If he were not in earnest, the kindest thing to do for him was to make him conscious that he was not. Therefore our Lord did not hesitate to put the condition of discipleship in the form that would most sharply test the depth and sovereignty of the "will to be perfect." The thin veneer of noble aspiration fell away, and the solid basis of worldly and self-regarding worldliness stood confessed. So much the better for the man; for now that he knew what to do, and that his wealth was the hindrance to his doing it, there was some possibility that present refusal might lead to searchings of heart, and that at a future time he might be ready to accept as a joy what he now shrank from as too great a sacrifice. We may be sure that the love which laid down the conditions did not turn away from him when he recoiled from them, nor cease to follow the young heart which had been touched with real though imperfect longings, though its owner ceased for the moment to follow Jesus. Still He looks with love on such hearts, and still His best gift to them is the clear call to full surrender, in which alone they will find the satisfaction of their desires, and be the objects of His yet tenderer love.

IV. We note, finally, Christ bowed down under the burden of the world's sin.

We turn lastly to Mark's account of Gethsemane, concerning which the less we say the less shall we err. "Put off thy shoes from off thy feet." Cold analysis is out of place, but a reverent word or two may be permitted. We get a glimpse of Jesus beneath the olives by the quivering moonlight, as one may see by a lightning-flash through the darkness of storm a labouring ship out on a wild sea. Mark employs two words to indicate Christ's emotions at that dread hour. "Greatly amazed" is perhaps scarcely strong enough to modern ears to represent the mental condition intended, since *astonishment* has encroached on *bewilderment*, which is the true idea of "amazed." "Appalled" or "stupefied" would probably convey the meaning more clearly. The other expression is better given by the Revised Version as "sore troubled" than by the Authorized Version's "very heavy." To these two pathetic words we have to add our Lord's own unique acknowledgment of weakness and appeal for sympathy, "My soul is exceeding sorrowful, even unto death," in which the word rendered "exceeding sorrowful" suggests the image of sorrows as ringing Him round in an unbroken circle. That strong expression, "unto death," must not be weakened into a mere superlative, but taken in its literal force as implying that the grief was all but fatal. One turn more of the rack and actual death would have ensued. Well may such a state be called, as it is by Luke, "agony."

Now we may reverently ask what it was which thus

appalled and all but crushed Him, and we shall answer the question most unworthily and inadequately if we suppose that it was merely the apprehension of approaching death. Such an explanation dishonours Him, putting Him lower in fortitude than many of His servants, who have drawn their calmness in the prospect and actual suffering of martyrdom from Him; and it is transparently insufficient. A far heavier weight than that pressed Him down, even the burden of the sins of the whole world, which then met on Him, not only because, in His perfect sympathy and self-oblivion, He identified Himself with sinful men, but also because, in a manner which we cannot explain but must accept, if we would do justice to Scripture teaching, "the Lord made to meet on Him the iniquity of us all." Unless the element of vicarious suffering entered into that mysterious agony, it will be very hard to account for it in any manner which will save the character of Jesus from disadvantageous comparisons with that of many a saint, hero, and sage. Socrates with his hemlock-cup, and not a few other dying men, are far nobler persons than this shuddering Suppliant beneath the trembling olives, unless His agony was caused by something much deeper than the natural recoil of the living from death. The world for nearly nineteen centuries has bowed in reverence before that pathetic picture of Christ in Gethsemane. Why? Be it reverently said, that unless the picture shows us "the Lamb of God, which taketh away the sin of the world," it shows us a very weak man, unmanned by what thousands have faced far better than He did.

Such are the glimpses which this evangelist affords of that infinite heart. It is full to-day of all the tenderness and pitying love which filled it in that past. It bled and ached for us while it beat on earth, and it still wells over with fellow-feeling for the sorrows, and pitying disapproval of the sins, of each of us. Some shade of sadness perhaps flits across even the joy of the Lord, when His brethren, whom He loved to the death, turn from His love, and it may still be possible for us to grieve Him. Be that as it may, He loves and pities all. Each may say, "He loves me, and I have a place in that heart." Let us turn our eyes to behold and our hearts to love that sum of all beauty and infinite mine of all human and Divine perfection made known to us in the heart of Jesus. The glimpses which we have into it here are blessedness. To know it fully is heaven.

GATHERED IN PEACE.

GATHERED IN PEACE.

"Behold, I will gather thee to thy fathers, and thou shalt be gathered to thy grave in peace."—2 CHRON. xxxiv. 28.

"The archers shot at King Josiah; and the king said unto his servants, Have me away; for I am sore wounded. . . . And they brought him to Jerusalem, and he died."—2 CHRON. xxxv. 23, 24.

IN these two passages we have a prophecy and its fulfilment. The event seems strangely unlike the prediction, "I will gather thee to thy fathers in peace." Is that fulfilled by the keen arrow, and the blood dropping from the king's heart on the floor of the chariot, and the premature death? Even so. Josiah, the King of Judah, to whom these words were spoken, and in whose death they were so strangely accomplished, had been smitten by the sudden discovery of the departure of himself and his nation from the precepts of the book of the Law, which had been found during the restoration of the neglected temple. It is not my purpose to enter at all on the questions of present interest connected with that discovery. Whatever that book was, and whether, as is thought by many now, those who hid knew where to find, the effect produced on the king was horror and penitence. He bade his advisers "inquire of the Lord" for him and his diminished people "concerning the words of this book"—apparently whether there was possibility of averting its threatenings. Remarkably, the godly counsellors turned at once to a woman, the wife of an inferior officer, who seems to have been principally known as his father's son, and from Huldah the prophetess they received the answer of which our first text is part. The judgments on the nation were declared irreversible, but the penitence of the king opened a way for his individual safety. Threatening and pardon were both revealed in the answer. Because Josiah's heart was tender, and he had humbled himself before God, therefore the mitigation announced in the former of our texts should be extended to him. Then, some twelve or fourteen years after, came the bloody death in battle, which seems to give the lie to the prophetess's assurance. It is worth while to lay the two side by side and gather the lessons of the juxtaposition.

I. We may first notice how these two passages of Scripture disclose the true Worker at the centre of things.

"*I* will gather thee," says God, speaking through Huldah. We turn the page, and where do we see His hand in the story of vulgar motives and godless strife? Josiah's death came about as "naturally" as possible, as the sequel of conflicts with which he had nothing directly to do. The chronic strife between Egypt and the kingdoms to the north of Judah had broken out again. This time the reigning Pharaoh was on his march against the strong Carchemish, which has recently, after so many millenniums of eclipse, become more than a name to us. He had no quarrel with Josiah, who seems to have pushed himself into the strife quite unnecessarily, with wrong-headed haste and obstinacy, in spite of the dignified and kindly remonstrances of the King of Egypt. The latter asserts his Divine commission, which he does not trace to any Egyptian deity, but to "God," and which he warns Josiah, as a worshipper of God, from opposing to his own ruin. The Chronicler endorses Pharaoh's claim, and declares his words to have been "from the mouth of God." So God sought to stay Josiah from the rashness which was to be his ruin, even though that ruin was determined, and determined to be effected by that act. Men are the authors of their own fall, and if they rush to their deaths, it is by their own obstinacy, in spite of Divine warnings. God can speak through a heathen king's lips, and good counsel has ever its source in Him, whatever be its channel. But if Josiah will be obstinate, and mix himself up in a quarrel which is not his, God works out His purposes through even the obstinacy of one man and the ambitions of another. Then came the fatal skirmish on that plain of Megiddo, which has run with blood so often from the days of Deborah and Barak down to almost our own, and perhaps has not yet heard for the last time "the noise of the captains and the shouting," nor seen Kishon sending a reddened current to the sea. The poor precaution of a disguise availed nothing for the hapless king. The archer's bow drawn at a venture sent an unaimed arrow, which a Divine hand directed, into his side. Lifted into a spare chariot, he lived over the jolting and agony of a swift flight to Jerusalem, and there died—one of the best of the kings of Judah, mourned by a nation's tears, and having thrown away his life out of pure wilfulness.

And all this play of commonplace motives—Pharaoh's pugnacity, Josiah's obstinacy, the forgotten politics of two empires, the chance arrow of an unconscious archer—is the fulfilment of that word, "*I* will gather thee to thy fathers." Is not this a penetrating glance beneath the whirling surface? Sometimes one sees on a swift river a tiny whirlpool, opening a pit an inch or two deep into the tawny raging flood. So here is, as it were, an eddy in the stream, that goes down to the very bottom and shows us the bed. We look through the cross-play of human purposes and acts, which are in themselves cognizant of nothing more than themselves, and discern what is really at work, determining their flow, and dashing one against the other or blending them in smooth flow.

Now, we say that we believe this and regard it as such a commonplace, that it is scarcely worth my while to repeat it, or yours to listen to it. But do we carry that steady eye which looks through all the play of so-called causes, and discerns God's hand in them all? Is it a living, ever-present conviction with us, influencing all our lives and thoughts? If we really believed it—and we do not really believe anything that is not present with us, shaping our habitual thinking—how different everything else would look! It is easy for us to set metaphysical puzzles. Any quantity of such may be picked up anywhere. But the old thought, which is here illustrated anew, has practical and devotional uses so manifold and valuable that we cannot afford to dismiss it as a commonplace. Commonplaces have to be reiterated till they are incorporated with the web of our thoughts, far more thoroughly than this one has yet become in the case of any of us. Not till we habitually see a present God working everywhere, and all things become transparent to His light, shining through them to our eyes, can we afford to put aside this truth as threadbare. If it ruled in us as it should do, how it would nourish faith and stimulate effort; how it would strengthen resignation and unreluctant submission; how it would deliver from vain and weakening regrets; how it would keep us from being angry with anything, or fretted with carking cares which gnaw at the very seat of life! If we saw God working everywhere and always, we should not be jaded with futile effort, nor disappointed or despairing, nor should we live among the tombs of a dead and buried past, and be blind to the worth of the living present. If we heard God speaking through all voices and sounds, whether of tempest and thunder, or of harpers harping with their harps, and saw His mighty hand moving all that moves, and His will dominant in all, fear would be far from us, and sorrow would wear a benignant cheer, and in our hearts would dwell the great peace, which is the dower of him who says, "It is the Lord; let Him do what seemeth Him good." Let us pray and strive for the clear and constant vision which looks through the things seen, which are but recipients and transmitters of power, to the energy which they receive and transmit. "I will gather thee to thy fathers," though the instruments be thine own obstinacy, the conflict of heathen powers, and the arrow of an ignorant bowman, who aimed at nothing, and never knew that he had killed a king and executed a Divine sentence.

II. There is, further, in these words a glimpse, though it be but dim, into the regions beyond the grave.

The two expressions in the former of these texts are by no means synonymous. "I will gather thee to thy fathers" is one thing; "Thou shalt be gathered to thy grave in peace" is quite another. The former phrase seldom occurs in the Old Testament, and never is found in the New. It appears principally in the Pentateuch, and in the closely related Book of Judges, and in these is found in a slightly different form, namely, "gathered to thy people" instead of "to thy fathers." It is used in that shape in reference to the deaths of Abraham, Isaac, Jacob, Ishmael, Aaron, and Moses. The generation contemporary with Joshua are spoken of as being "gathered to their fathers," and the same expression is employed in our text and in the parallel in 2 Kings. The variation of "people" and "fathers" is natural. The former phrase is applied to the fathers themselves, beyond whom the vision of their descendants did not travel backwards, whereas the latter is fitting when applied to later generations, to whom union with the venerable ancestors of the nation was honour. Now, this "gathering to thy people" or "thy fathers" is distinctly separated from both death and burial. The account of the last days of Abraham (Gen. xxv. 8) is a fair specimen of all the narratives in which this expression occurs, and in it three stages are clearly distinguished: "Abraham gave up the ghost, and died . . . and was gathered to his people. And Isaac and Ishmael his sons buried him." The lonely tomb on Mount Hor did not hinder Aaron's being gathered to his people, nor did the mysterious burial on Nebo shut out Moses from their society. That conception of accession to the great company somewhere is no mere euphemism for death, and still less refers to what may afterwards befall the body of the dead man. If, then, we are led, in all honesty of interpretation, to exclude both death and burial from the meaning of the phrase, what remains but to regard it as a faint gleam of insight into the condition, after death and burial, of the true self, which passes through death undying, and is not laid to moulder with the disused garment of flesh? The Cuneiform inscriptions have taught us how developed the doctrine of a future life was in Abraham's native country, and there is nothing improbable now in ascribing some share in that knowledge to Israel, however faint the traces of it in Scripture. To see in this remarkable phrase the conception of a future social life is not to read later ideas into a vague expression, which we make unnecessarily definite, but not to see that thought in it seems rather to evacuate it of its true significance. There is no doubt a danger, against which we are abundantly warned, of committing the anachronism of reading the results of later Revelations into the earlier records; but there is also a danger, which is less often insisted upon, of reading out of the earlier Revelations what is really in them, and of thus exaggerating the ignorance of early ages.

Surely this sweet and pathetic expression did spring from, and did suggest, some conceptions of a life beyond life, in which those who have lived solitary here should be knit together in a great company. In the earlier form the phrase held forth the hope that, after death, the desert wanderers should join the community to which they belonged, and from which they had been parted in life. In its later form, as in our text, it gave the hope that the descendants of the ancestors who had become august and sacred by lapse of time should be set with these venerated heroes and patriarchs of the nation, and that there should be, somehow and somewhere, as it were a great family home with many mansions, where the kindred of the fathers should dwell. The principle of the anticipated association seems to have been purely that of natural kinship. The children of Abraham were to be gathered round him, a happy clan in that dim world. Beyond these two ideas of society and repose, the hope expressed in this phrase apparently did not soar.

But we may use the earlier and inadequate phrase as the vehicle of our deeper conceptions and higher hopes. We too have to look forward to a state where, "in solemn troops and sweet societies," souls that have toiled weary and lonely through the changeful desert of this life, shall find at last rest and companionship, and shall "sit down with Abraham and Isaac and Jacob in the kingdom" of the great Father of all. The earlier hope is translated into a loftier, for we know that the principle of association in that solemn, blessed state, where perfect society is realized by hearts isolated in life, is not that of natural but of spiritual affinity, and that there the same law of like to like, which binds happy souls to their Lord and to one another, shall knit other spirits alien from these into a dark confraternity of repulsion and yet of contiguity.

Here and now men are grouped by other uniting forces, but hereafter spiritual character shall determine company and sphere, and each shall find himself surrounded by the environment of persons and circumstance for which he has fitted himself. "What maketh heaven, that maketh hell." That is manifoldly true, and this is one sphere in which it holds. "Being let go, they went unto their own company." When set free from the disturbing influences of life here, men will arrange themselves according to character. The stones on the eternal shore will lie in order, as on some beaches we see the heavier blocks laid in long rows and the lighter ranged together, and then the sand. The tide has sorted them. Life classifies and aggregates men, and yonder they are with their likes. So Judas "went to his own place," wherever that may have been. He passed into the sphere fitted for him, and there found others. A solemn law of spiritual affinity as determining the future associations of each lies hid in the old words, "I will gather thee to thy fathers," and still more clearly in the other form of the saying, "He was gathered to his people."

The former expression suggests, too, the hope of personal communion with the venerable names whose spiritual children we smaller men are proud to call ourselves. A community implies communication, and a gathering together of spirits which forbade intercourse would be no gathering; for spirits are not together by juxtaposition, but by intercourse and affinity. It would be easy to let fancy run wild in pictures of that intercourse, and to summon up a long list of glorious names; but the fact itself is more than all our ignorant amplifications of it, and the vividness of expectation does not increase with the increase of imaginative details, which smother rather than enforce the truth. It is enough to believe that those who are united to the same Lord shall form a real unity, which necessarily includes communication. The future is set forth as a city. Are the citizens not to exchange thought and feeling by some better means than words, our imperfect medium here? They shall dwell in deep peace, encompassed by congenial natures, and delivered from the lifelong torture of grating against harsh contraries of their truest selves. While they are in the midst of their own people, in that they are surrounded with those like them, they shall be gathered to their fathers, in that they will be capable of association with those who excel them in strength, and are before them in spiritual stature. The whole blissful company shall partake of a common progress, yet retaining the individuality of its separate parts and the unity of the whole, like some cloud saturated with sunshine, and slowly drifting nearer the sun. The loftiest will be the helpful companions of the lowliest. The unity of life in each will forbid the diverse degrees of life from becoming barriers. In that blessed society will be both impulse and rest. The same law will work in darker fashion in souls that are void of that Christ-derived life; but there likeness will bring no repose, and the community of alienation from God will ensure no community of friendship among the alienated. It is conceivable that such aggregation may be worse than solitude or than hostile neighbourhood; for companions in evil here are not friends, and yonder the same result may follow in an intenser degree. There may be a kingdom, but a kingdom of anarchy. There may be similarity in the fundamental relation to God, along with fierce antagonism and repulsion otherwise. One awe-struck glance is all permitted us, and it shows us how this principle of association according to character in a future world, may be as a fountain doing what James said that no fountain could do, sending forth both sweet waters and bitter.

The word rendered "gather" is often employed for the action of the reaper or of him who collects fruits. May we not blend some such allusion with its use here? It is God who says, "I will gather thee," and there is tenderness and care in the word. That last parting from the familiar things of earth is no violent dragging away, but the act of the great Husbandman, who plucks the ripe fruit because it is precious to Him. Sentiment talks of Death as the reaper, but the antique simplicity of our text goes far deeper than that representation. Not Death, but God, is the Reaper. Death is only His sickle. It is He who gathers in His sheaves and stores them in His great storehouse.

III. Finally, we may see here a discovery of the true sphere of peace.

Was Huldah one of the juggling prophetesses who palter with a double sense, keeping a promise in some fashion and yet breaking it? So it might seem to one looking at the poor young king in his chariot, faint with loss of blood and fleeing from the fatal field. Was this being "gathered to his fathers in peace"? If the prophecy was fulfilled thus, what would non-fulfilment be? The fact looks like a flat contradiction of the promise, and so prosaic commentators have puzzled themselves as to how to reconcile the two. But surely there is no mystery in the matter, and the reconcilement of the apparent contradiction is easy, as is so often the case, if we understand the meaning of the words employed. For what does God's Spirit mean by "peace"? Surely something deeper and more inward and inwrought with the substance of the soul than the mere absence of outward strife and battle. The peace which was promised to Josiah was maintained whether or no Pharaoh-Necho's soldiers stormed across Palestine, and the arrows flew thick on the plain of Jezreel.

Such a promise so fulfilled is meant to teach us the great truth for life and for death, that true peace does not depend on the absence of tumult, but on the presence of God. It is an attribute of the soul, not of circumstances, and is often more fully possessed in conflict than in calm. They who look for it in any conjunction of outward good, search for it in the wrong place. If it live not in the heart of the seeker, he seeks it in vain, and it lives only in the heart where God abides. The foot of Christ is the only charm to still the heaving billows, and round Him, as He moves in the greatness of His strength across the wild ocean, is an atmosphere of calm. If we pass into it, the wildest storm will not ruffle a fluttering garment or lift a light hair. We may carry our own weather with us through all storms, and dwell in the peace of God, as in a fortress, though enemies rage around. "In the world ye shall have tribulation, but in Me ye shall have peace." The outward life in the world must be disturbed, harassed, beset in a hundred ways by strifes and annoyances; but the true life which is rooted in Jesus Christ, by faith, and love, and desire, and obedience, may all the while be the seat of holy calm, as some still oratory in the centre of a beleaguered castle. To be "in Christ" is to be "in peace."

In like manner, the fulfilment of this prophecy in the death of Josiah referred not to the outward fashion of his dying, but to the composure and resignation of spirit, not haply without some foregleams of a great assemblage of saints to welcome his coming, with which he passed hence. As for the outward fact, the fierce current of the fight, the shout of battle, the agony and flight, were very unlike what the recipient of the promise may have expected; but may not his death have been as peaceful there as if in the seclusion of his palace, amid careful tending? Not the curtained chamber, the loving hands to smooth the pillow, or any of the other alleviations of the last conflict, make it death "in peace." That is secured only by the same thing as secures the like blessing for life—even the presence of God in Christ, realized by faith. Many of us may have seen the horrible frescoes in a church in Rome, where all varieties of cruel martyrdoms are grossly pictured. "These all died in faith," and if they did, they died in peace, though nameless tortures wrung their poor frames. Virgins whose blood reddened the sands of the amphitheatre, confessors wrapped in pitch and set flaming in Cæsar's garden, martyrs stretched on the rack or burned at the stake, died, according to the estimate of sense, in agony and tumult which it would be foolish to call peace; but according to the estimate of God, which is the ultimate truth and reality of things, their deaths were but as the peaceful harvesting of the shock of corn fully ripe. The first Christian martyr, crushed by the heavy stones flung by fanatic hands, and kneeling outside the city wall in a pool of his own blood, died so peacefully that the only word to describe his gentle departure is, "he fell asleep," like a tired child on its mother's lap.

So this King of Israel, smitten between the joints of his armour by the keen Egyptian arrow, was by battle brought to his grave in peace. So we, whatever be the circumstances attending our passage from this death which we call life into the life which men call death, may meet them and pass through them with quiet hearts, and have peace as well as hope in our death.

Let us understand the deep meaning of the great promise of peace, which this story obliges us to recognize, and we shall see in the apparent contradiction its real fulfilment, and gain a lesson very profitable for life and for death. If, living, we live unto the Lord, and dying, die unto Him, and so, living and dying, are the Lord's, then, living or dying, we shall keep and be kept in His last gift of perfect peace, which shall not be broken by any of the tumults of life or the terrors and tempests of death.

SOME REASONS WHY THE WORD BECAME FLESH.

SOME REASONS WHY THE WORD BECAME FLESH.

"He is not ashamed to call them brethren, saying, I will declare Thy name unto My brethren, in the midst of the Church will I sing praise to Thee. And again, I will put My trust in Him. And again, Behold I and the children which God hath given Me."—HEB. ii. 11-13.

"ASHAMED to call them brethren"—why should He be? It is no condescension to acknowledge the fact of brotherhood with humanity, any more than it is humiliation to be born. But there was a Man who emptied and humbled Himself by being "found in fashion as a man," and for whom it was infinite condescension to call us His brethren. We can say of a prince that he is not ashamed to call his subjects friends, and to sit down to eat with them, but it would be absurd to say so of one of the subjects in reference to his fellows. The full, lofty truth of the first chapter of this Epistle underlies that word "ashamed," which is meaningless unless Jesus was the "effulgence of the Father's glory, and the very image of His substance." Only on that understanding are His birth and enrolment of Himself among us men the transcendent instances of His loving self-abasement.

The writer quotes three Old Testament passages which

he regards as prophetic of our Lord's identifying of Himself with humanity.

It is no part of my present purpose to inquire into the principles on which the writer asserts the Messianic reference of the passages quoted. I desire rather to point out that these three cited sayings deal with three different aspects of our Lord's manhood, and of the purpose of His incarnation, and that, therefore, they unitedly give, if not a complete, yet a comprehensive answer to the question, Why did God become Man? The first of them shows us our Lord assuming manhood in order to declare God to men; the second gives the purpose of His incarnation as being the providing of a Pattern of the devout life for men; and the third presents it as being the bringing of men into the relationship of sons.

I. Jesus is Man that He may declare God to men.

The first quotation in our text is taken from that psalm whence our Lord drew the awful words which pierced the darkness and broke the silence as He hung on the cross, "My God, My God, why hast Thou forsaken Me?" The psalm springing directly from the heart of one sorely afflicted (whether David or another, and whether the sufferer be the ideal of the nation or no, matter nothing for the purpose of the writer of the Epistle), and referring in the consciousness of the psalmist to his own feelings in the midst of his sorrows, has yet been so moulded into language a world too wide for the psalmist's case, and corresponding in a number of minute details—such as the parting of the vesture by lot, the piercing of the hands and feet, and the mockery of the passers-by—with the facts of the crucifixion, that we cannot fail to perceive the figure of the Man of sorrows, the Prince of all the afflicted, shimmering through the words of the single sufferer who pours out his plaint in the psalm, whether he himself was conscious or no that his words portrayed anything more than his own misery. Every true mourner's cries fit the lips of every other, and every lesser sorrow may be regarded as a miniature of the greatest, which is Christ's. But in these laments of the psalmist we shall miss their deepest pathos unless we recognize something more than this mere general correspondence of grief with grief, heart answering to heart, deep answering to deep across the ages, because all hearts are alike, and hear in them the tones of prophecy speaking through the possibly unconscious psalmist. The words quoted in our text are those in which he grasps in faith the certainty of deliverance, and vows that, delivered, he will magnify his delivering God among his brethren. Sorrow had driven him to supplication. Supplication and sorrow had brought deliverance. The experience of all three had fitted him to speak with fuller assurance and insight of the Name of God, and thankfulness for all had put a new song into the lips that had groaned and prayed. Therefore his thankfulness must needs pass into proclamation to all around of what God would do, and in the estimate of faith had already done, for his soul, even while sorrow pressed on him.

And is not this true of Jesus and of His earthly life? Was He not made perfect by suffering, not indeed in regard of His own moral nature, but in reference to His fitness to be the Author of eternal salvation to us? His fullest declaration of the Father's name was only possible after and by reason of His sufferings and ascended glory, as He Himself has taught us when He prayed, and said, "I have declared Thy name, and will declare it."

What, then, is this office of declaring the name of the

Father? That name is not the mere syllables by which men address God, but is the manifested character, as always in Scripture. Therefore the declaration of it must be by acts more than by words. And so the highest revelation of God must be by a human life. A personal God can only be revealed by a person. He can only be shown to men by a life. Words, however beautiful, tender, true, and self-evidencing, will not suffice. They represent men's thinkings, but they can never certify God's fact. They may suggest hopes, fears, peradventures; but unless we have a living person, whose deeds on the plain level of history are the manifestation of God, our thoughts of Him will neither be solid with certainty nor sweet with healing and comfort. Our highest conceptions of God must be moulded after the analogy of the only spiritual existence of which we have experience, namely, the human, and the anthropomorphism, against which we are often solemnly warned, is a necessity of thought, and in its purest forms is the most worthy idea of the infinite God. It may be gross or refined, but it is inevitable. Man was made in the image of God, and that fact guarantees the truth of the conceptions of God which think of His infinite perfection as the reality of which our limited and stained manhood is yet the image, distorted and diminished though it be. The analogy is such, that the brightness of the Father's glory can be mirrored and manifested in a human life. The life of Jesus is the making visible for men of the glory of the invisible God.

The human life that reveals God must be more than human. It is not enough for us to think of Jesus as revealing God in the manner in which saints have done. Only when we believe in His Divinity does His humanity assume for us revealing power.

What is the substance of His declaration of God? The "attributes," as they are called, of supreme Being, such as omniscience, omnipotence, and other majestic appendages of Divinity, which are the opposites of the characteristics of finite humanity, are but superficial, not of the essence of the Name. They are but the fringe of the light; the central brightness is a milder light than blazes in these. High above these forms of power, tower the moral attributes of purity and righteousness. But when we have passed through the outer court of the former and the holy place of the latter, there is yet a veil to be lifted, and within it there is a mercy-seat, and above it the still presence of the Glory, filling the shrine with uncoruscating rays of lambent light. God is Power. That has been the belief and the dread of the world from of old. God is Righteousness. That has been the faith of purer souls, and the half-stifled witness of conscience. God is Love. That is the new message which Christ has brought by something better than saying so, even by living that gentle life of pity, and dying that death of sacrifice, and telling us, for the interpretation of both, "He that hath seen Me hath seen the Father." God has wisdom, power, eternal Being, and so on; but God is Love. These other mighty things are but the "attributes" of the love which is Himself.

All other means of knowing God are imperfect. Nature gives but ambiguous responses, and while "the earth is full of the goodness of the Lord," it is no less true that much in it seems to speak of either malignant or thwarted beneficent power, and might well be the support of dualism or of atheism. Nature needs to be interpreted in the light of Christ's revelation of God before it yields clear evidence of the love of God. History and our own intuitions do little to supply the deficiency. These, and all other sources apart from Christ, are like the fragmentary inscriptions in some ruined temple, from which may be pieced together, by much pains and at much risk of error, some more or less incomplete and illegible records of the gods once enshrined there. But the whole name is in Jesus Christ given for reading by the least learned, in whom all the syllables which were uttered at sundry times and divers manners, and of which the broken echoes have been reverberating confusedly in men's ears, are gathered into one majestic full-toned Name. All other sources of knowledge of God fail in certainty. They yield only assertions which may or may not be true. At the best, we are relegated to peradventures and guesses and theories if we turn away from Jesus Christ. Men said that there was land away across the Atlantic for centuries before Columbus went and brought back its products. He discovers who proves. Christ has not merely spoken to us beautiful and sacred things about God, as saint, philosopher, or poet might do, but He has shown us God; and henceforward, to those who receive Him, the Unknown Root of all being is not a hypothesis, a great Perhaps, a dread or a hope, as the case may be, but the most certain of all facts, of Whom and of whose love we may be surer than we can be of aught besides but our own being.

If Jesus Christ has not declared God's name to His brethren, we have no knowledge of that name. It is becoming more and more plain with every day that the tendencies of thought now are bringing us full front with this alternative—either Jesus Christ or none. Either He has shown us God, and in His light we see light, or we are left to grope in the dark. Either God is manifested in

Him, or there is no manifestation at all. Unless "the only begotten Son, which is in the bosom of the Father, hath declared Him," no man hath seen God at any time. Deism or Theism will not sustain itself against the corrosion of the acid of the modern spirit. Men may reject Christ's revelation of God, and still say, "We think, "We hope," or "We fear"; but they cannot say, "We know," unless they accept His "Verily, verily, I say unto you." Either He has shown us God, or God is a mere sound which tells little and assures of less. The educated mind of England is confronted with this choice—either God manifest in the flesh; or a God who is at the best "a stream of tendency not ourselves, that makes for righteousness;" or a great unknown somewhat, of whom, or rather of which, we know only that it cannot be known. From all these cheerless and nebulous thoughts we turn to Jesus, and as we hear Him saying, "I will declare Thy name unto My brethren," we see the sun again instead of the doleful grey that veiled our sky, and regain a God who loves and pities; a God of whom we can be certain; a God who has an ear, a heart, and a hand; a God whom in Christ, and in Christ alone, we can know, and whom to know is life eternal.

II. Jesus is Man that He may show to men the life of devout trust.

"And again, I will put My trust in Him." This quotation is from Isa. viii. The prophet, like the sufferer in the former passage, speaks his own devout dependence on God, apparently with no consciousness of any prophetic reference in his words. Our writer sees in Isaiah a foreshadowing of Jesus. The whole prophetic order was a prophecy of *the* Prophet. This prophet, exalted as he was to declare the will of God, at a crisis of the nation's history, standing before his generation in the fulness of inspiration, feels himself not absolved from the necessity of devout dependence on God. That sense of dependence and exercise of faith are part of the prophetic ideal. He who declares God's name to his brethren must share with his brethren the emotions of personal religion, which may all be summed up in that one of trust or faith.

This, too, is true of Jesus. He is one of us, and His brotherhood is shown in that He too lived the life which He lived in the flesh by faith in God. He is not only the Object, but also the Pattern, of faith. Many orthodox believers in the Divinity of our Lord are too much afraid of giving due weight to that aspect of His manhood. There is much confusion in many minds, in which there is no proper belief either in Christ's true manhood or in His proper Divinity, but only in a strange amalgam of both, in which each element neutralizes to some extent the characteristics of the other. Hence men who do see clearly the real humanity of Jesus and nothing more, will shatter such perplexed belief.

Perfect manhood is dependent manhood. A reasonable creature who does not live by faith is a monster arrogating the prerogative of God, and therein assuming the likeness of the devil. Christ's perfect manhood did not release Him from, but bound Him to, the exercise of faith. Nor did His true Deity make faith impossible to His manhood. Christ's perfect manhood perfected His faith, and in some aspects modified it. His trust had no relation to the consciousness of sin, and no element either of repentance or of longing for pardon. But it had relation to the consciousness of need, and was in Him, as in us, the condition of continual derivation of life and power from the Father. Himself has said, "I live through the Father," and the indwelling Divinity of the Son did not make superfluous the influx of the Father's life into His manhood by the channel of faith. His faith was unlike ours, in that it was steady. Our hands tremble with the very pulses of our blood, as we hold the telescope which shows us the things not seen. His hand knew no tremor or perturbation from throbbing flesh, and no mist dimmed His vision. Our faith is often interrupted, and is like an intermittent spring. His was a perennial flow.

Christ's perfect faith brought forth perfect fruits in His life, issuing, as it did, in obedience which was perfect in purity of motive, in gladness of submission, and in completeness of the resulting deeds as well as in its continuity, through His life. "I do always the things that please Him," was His own summing up of His activity. Was that arrogant and ignorant self-satisfaction, or the true utterance of a manhood which, in its absolute non-participation in the universal consciousness of defect and transgression, stands unique, and demands the supposition of something more than manhood in Him? That perfect faith further issued in unbroken communion. Like two metal plates of which the surfaces are so true that when brought together they adhere, the Father and the Son were inseparably united, in the trustful and obedient consciousness of Jesus.

Thus our Lord not only comes among us to show us God, but also to show us the true glory and strength of man, and to let us see how Divine a thing our nature may be made when it is knit to the Divine by faith. He teaches us the possibilities of faith, both in itself and in its ennobling effect on life. Out of His example we may take both shame and encouragement—shame when we measure our poor, purblind, feeble, and interrupted faith against His, and encouragement when we raise our hopes to the height of the revelation in it of what ours may become. The staff that He leaned on He has bequeathed to us, who still travel the rough road where His footprints are yet visible. The shield which He bore, unpierced and undinted by all the fiery darts that struck it, He has left for us to brace on our arms. The Captain and Perfecter of faith was once in the arena where we wrestle and fight. He conquered because He ever said, "I will put My trust in Him;" and we too shall be victors, if we look away from all besides, and up to Him where He now sits enthroned, the object and the pattern of our trust. "This is the victory that overcometh the world, even our faith."

III. Jesus is Man that He may bring men into the family of sons of God.

"Behold I and the children which God hath given Me." These words are taken from the immediate context of the last quotation. In their original application, the prophet speaks of himself and of his family, and of the little group of disciples who had been drawn to him, as being associated with him as God's witnesses—the salt of the nation, which but for them would perish in its rottenness. The writer of the Epistle sees in that Israel within Israel a shadow of the New Testament Church, and in the prophet's humility, which united these little ones, who had received natural life or spiritual impulse from him, with himself in his prophetic office, some hint of the greater condescension of Christ, who in like manner bestows life on those who trust Him, and lifts them to a wondrous participation in His Sonship to God and in His work for men. We can scarcely say that this quotation stands on the same level as the first of the passages quoted. It gives an illustration rather than an actual type or prophecy, and is analogy rather than purposed foreshadowing. The change from "brethren," as in the first quotation, to "children" is to be noticed. Isaiah was parent, and "the children" were partly his family and partly his followers. Christians receive spiritual life from Christ, but God is the Father and Christ is the elder Brother. "Children" does not refer to relationship in the same sphere as "brethren" does. The latter means kindred by a common manhood; the former, kindred by possession of the same spiritual life. While Christ is Source of spiritual life for us, He Himself lives through the Father; and since the paradox that the Father hath *given* Him to have life *in Himself* is true, the more common representation of brotherhood with Him and this of sonship are equally in accordance with the facts. We have, then, presented in this final clause, the effect of the Incarnation as being power to us to become sons of God. The three clauses of our text give a regular progress of idea. Christ becomes Man to show us God. In His humanity He lives, like us, by faith. The result of his identifying Himself with us as our Brother is that we are identified with Him as children of God. The former clauses dealt with Christ's becoming like us, this with our becoming like Him.

Our Lord, then, becomes Man that through Him men may receive a new life which is His own. That impartation of a new Divine life is the deepest truth and the richest gift of the gospel. Do not be satisfied with any less conception of what God gives us in the unspeakable gift of His Son than this, that He therein gives to all who accept Jesus in faith a spark of His own life, which will transform our deadness into quick and joyous sensibility and activity worthy of its source. But for that gift of life more than incarnation is needed. Jesus Christ can only impart His life on condition of His death. The alabaster box must be broken, though so precious, and though the light of the pure spirit within shone lustrous and softened through it, in order that the house may be filled with the odour of the ointment. By His death He puts Death to death, and takes away the hindrances to the bestowal of the true life.

Again, He becomes Man that men may, by the communication of His life, become sons of God. Since He is the Son, those who receive life from Him enter thereby into the relationship of sons. They are God's children, being Christ's brethren. They are brought into a new unity, and being members of one family are one by a sacreder oneness than the possession of a common humanity. The brotherhood of men will only become a reality to which men's institutions and sentiments will correspond, when it rests on the fatherhood of God, realized through faith in that elder Brother, who grudges nothing to the prodigal sons, but Himself has come to seek them and bring them back.

Further, Jesus is Man that men may become sharers in His prerogatives and offices. As Isaiah gathered his children and scholars into a family, and gave them to partake in his prophetic office, and to be "for signs and wonders," so Christ gathers us into marvellous oneness with Himself. He becomes like us in our lowliness and flesh of sin, that we may become like Him in His glory and perfection. The identification of Jesus and His disciples is represented in Scripture with extraordinary boldness, as being like the ineffable union of the Father with the Son; as being faintly shadowed by the vital relation of head and body; as being closer and more inward than the union of husband and wife, who are but "one flesh," while "he that is joined to the Lord is one spirit." Accordingly, the same names are applied to them and to Him. Is He the Light of the world? So are they. Is He the Anointed? So are they. The Christian Church is the prolongation of the life of Christ on earth, and while the great sacrifice which He has made once for all on the cross cannot be repeated, copied, or paralleled, and needs no repetition, there are aspects even of His sufferings in which His servants have to fill up their measure for the sake of the brethren. The union is as of the graft into the tree, with the difference that here it is not the good graft which is inserted in the wild stock, but the wild slip which is introduced into the good tree and partakes both of its root and fatness.

Further, Christ is Man that He may present His family at last to God. If we love and trust Him, He will hold us in His strong and tender grasp, and never part from us till He presents us at last faultless and joyful before the presence of His and our Father—

"No wanderer lost,
A family in heaven."

The sum of the whole matter is this. There is but one way of knowing God. All else is darkness and uncertainty, shifting as cloud-rack, and unsubstantial as it. God has spoken to us in the Son. If we see Christ, we see God. There is but one noble, peaceful, worthy life for man—a life of faith in Him, who is at once the Object and the Example of our faith, and believing in whom we believe in the Father also. There is but one fountain of life opened in this grave-yard of a world, of whose waters whosoever drinks shall "have in him a fountain of water springing up into everlasting life." There is but one way of becoming sons of God. Christ our Brother is the Revealer of God, the Pattern of devotion, the Source and Upholder of life. Listen to Him declaring the name of the Father. Put your trust in Him, for you trust in God when you have faith in Christ. Open your heart that His life may flow into your death. Then His strong hand will hold you up, and at last He will acknowledge you for His in the presence of the Father and of the holy angels, and will point to you, saved, glorified, and like Himself, with the triumphant words, "Behold I and the children whom God hath given Me."

ARMED RECREANTS.

ARMED RECREANTS.

"The children of Ephraim, being armed, and carrying bows, turned back in the day of battle."—Ps. lxxviii. 9.

THE great tribe of Ephraim was the principal constituent in the kingdom of Israel, and so important that the whole kingdom is frequently in Scripture called by the name of the tribe. Whether that be so here or no is difficult to determine, because the historical reference of our text is uncertain. It evidently points to some old, forgotten battle, of which we know nothing. But the psalm, as a whole, comes from the southern kingdom of Judah, and culminates in the triumphant celebration of God's rejection of the northern portion of the nation in favour of Judah, in which He set His tabernacle. The dereliction of duty expressed in my text seems to be suggested as one cause of the withdrawal of the Divine favour. What was that dereliction of duty? It is difficult to settle whether "turned back in the day of battle" means a cowardly flight from the field, being beaten, or a slothful and selfish refusal to go into the field and fight. Either idea would explain the language. But the emphasis which is put upon the thorough equipment of the soldiers, seems rather to favour the idea that what is meant by "turning back in the day of battle" is that these men, thus equipped with weapons for the fight, refused the fight for which they were equipped. And so, I think, we have in the words lessons that we may well lay to heart.

I. Note, then, first, the fact.

Now, the assertion here, when applied to us, is just this—that every Christian, by virtue of his Christianity, is sufficiently armed for the great conflict. We all have the gift of that Divine Spirit, who "will teach our hands to war and our fingers to fight." Jesus Christ imparts Himself to every soul that trusts Him; and "this is the victory that overcometh the world, even our faith." Then, in addition to the universal sufficient equipment which belongs to every Christian soul, there are also included the variety of gifts. In a great army such as Eastern despots used to gather, before military science had reached its present diabolical perfection, there were men armed in all sorts of fashions; the foremost ranks with spears and swords and bows, perhaps, the hindmost with clubs and sticks; but all with something in their hands with which they could strike a brave stroke for their king. And so all we Christian people, in the variety of our gifts, have sufficient weapons for the warfare, and sufficient tools for the tasks allotted to us. There are "diversities of administrations, but it is the same Lord;" and there are differences of gifts, but it is He that ministers to each and to all.

Then this is the fact that we, who, by virtue of our being Christian people, are sufficiently armed for offensive and defensive warfare and for victory, do yet to a terrible extent shirk the fight, let opportunities slip away unused, like so much water through slack hands, neglect to stir up the gift that is in us, and "being armed, and carrying bows," look at the serried ranks in front of us, and slink away out of the field, leaving who will to bear the brunt.

There are two phases of the warfare to which every Christian soul is summoned: the one is the fight with our own evil, which is not to be subdued merely by peaceful culture, but needs stern antagonism; and the other is the effort to spread the name of Jesus Christ, which is to be done not merely by the missionary work of proclamation, but also by warring against the evils that infest and hag-ride the world. These two branches of the one conflict are set before all Christian men; and all of us, more or less, have to take to ourselves the indictments of this text of ours, and to confess that, with our opportunities and equipments, our gifts and capacities and possessions, we have turned away in the day of battle.

Brother! who is there amongst us that has worked and fought up to the edge of his capacity? There is no more wasteful instrument, they tell us, than a steam-engine; so little motive power comes out for so much heat applied, and such a quantity is lost. So it is with us. All the warmth that radiates from Jesus Christ is poured into the icy deadness of the reservoirs of our hearts, and the effect is only to raise the temperature such a very little, and to get two or three feeble strokes of the piston. We hang our weapons on the wall, as they do in baronial mansions, for ornament, instead of taking them down for use. None of us can plead "not guilty" to the charge of neglected opportunities and unused powers, and talents hid in a napkin, and there are some of us to whom this charge of my text comes with a very special weight of accusation and condemnation. What a dead mass of idle people there are in every Christian congregation and Church! I do not mean merely those who do not take any part in the organized activities of the community to which they belong—that is for their conscience; but I mean that, professing themselves Christian men and women, and living in some feeble fashion as such, they yet do nothing with the forces entrusted to them, and have hardly any growth in godliness for themselves, and have seldom lifted a finger to do anything for Christ among men.

Ah! there are more non-effective soldiers in the roll-call of Christ's army than in that of any volunteer corps that was ever heard of; and at the musters there are a dreadful number "absent without leave," whose names might just as well be struck off the muster-roll altogether.

Another suggestion may be made here. The men that are best armed are very often the first to run away. It is by no means the fact that the rich man, for instance, is the large giver. It is by no means the fact that the relatively largely endowed man, with the greatest educational advantages or intellectual power, is the vigorous worker in the Church. It is generally the other way. The men that have the bows—which was the mightest instrument of warfare with Israel in those rude old days—are not the fighting-men.

These are generally the poor people in the back ranks, who have only sticks and knives, and make the best of their poor weapons, because they are more loyal to the King and Captain. Oh! you rich men, if there are any of you here; you clever people; you well-educated folk; you men and women with leisure; recognize that the endowment that distinguishes you from others is God's way of saying to you, "Go into My vineyard!" and let us al try that the charge of my text shall be less applicable to us.

II. Note, next, the black, deep guilt of this negative crime.

We are all quite ready to admit, and forward to plead, that inability absolves from duty. Do we ever remember, or do we remember as quickly when tasks present themselves, the converse, that ability prescribes duty? You cannot take the benefit of the excuse on the one hand unless you are ready to accept the obligation on the other. Power settles duty. "Can" and "ought" cover precisely the same ground to an inch, both in regard of manner and of measure. Ability settles the duty, and *obligation* is only another way of saying *capacity*. So, then, brethren, we come to this, that the negative refusal, so to speak, to go into the fight is positive treason. For what lies in it? What does a man who simply does *not* visit the imprisoned Christ, or bring consolation to His comfortless servants, or simply hides his talent in a napkin, and does not use it,—what does he do in his *not* doing? He betrays his Master, is disloyal to his King, is hurtful to himself and cruel to his fellows. And what I wish to urge upon you is this, that the negative fault that is charged in my text is a positive crime, of as deep and dark a dye as any Christian man can commit; and more dangerous, because more subtle, and less apparently perilous than many an act which looks a great deal worse. Negligence is enough to damn a man. In order to go down to the nethermost depths, you do not need to do anything; you have simply *not* to do something, and down you will go by gravitation. Although there may be nothing else to condemn a man at Christ's tribunal, do not forget that the worst condemnation that ever He spoke was directed in parable to a man who had no positive faults at all, or at least none that are named, and none that come into condemnation. He could apparently say and with perfect truth, as the Pharisee in the parable said, "I am not as other men are, extortioners, unjust, adulterers, or even as this publican." He was a member of the Church; he filled his place; nobody could say a word against him. Jesus Christ had nothing to say against him. All that was wrong with him was—what? That he took his talent, wrapped it up in a cloth, and hid it away somewhere. I wonder if there are any professing Christians here, blameless before the eyes of the world, blameless even before the tribunal of their own callous consciences, who live decent, respectable, orderly, law-abiding lives, up to the standard of Christian morality in a great many respects; only—only, "having bows, they turn back in the day of battle."

III. Now let me say a word about the reasons for this cruel, cowardly, and criminal dereliction of duty.

One of them is a want of honest study of ourselves in reference to our duty. Did you ever spend a quiet half-hour in thinking over what is really in your power, in order to ascertain what you are bound to do? Or do you take your forms of Christian service for others, and of Christian culture for yourselves, at haphazard, or by mere slavish imitation of other people? I believe that there are few parts of Christian culture more neglected by the average Christian people of this generation than the old-fashioned habit of self-examination; not in order to find out reasons for confidence—God forbid!—nor in order to find out reasons for diffidence either, but in order to find out paths of work, and to try and ascertain, by an examination of their own capacities, what are their duties. I believe that if you would do that habitually, prayerfully, in the sight of

God, your whole lives would be revolutionized, and your "profiting would appear unto all men."

There are a great many of us who are never so modest as when we are asked to work for Christ. It is then that we find out, and are ready to say, "Oh, I cannot do this, that, or the other thing." The discovery generally coincides with the appeal of apparent duty. So it is rather suspicious, is it not?

There is another very widely operative cause, namely, absorbing attention to and interest in selfish and transitory needs. Suppose these men of Ephraim had said, "Bows? Oh yes! we've got bows. We use them principally to shoot wild goats for our food. That is the employment of them that we find most profitable."

That is what many of us do with our capacities. The men are armed, and they are so busy, as sportsmen say, "shooting for the pot," that they have no time for the fight. A Christian who gives as much of his life's blood and his heart's energy as most of us do to the mere provision of external good has very little leisure to spare, and less freshness of spirit to consecrate to Jesus Christ. And although I know that the honest pursuit of daily bread is a first duty for heads of families, and is part of the "seeking of the kingdom of God and His righteousness," yet no man who has to preach the gospel in a great commercial centre can help seeing that to a far more than is needful extent, in multitudes of cases, the cares of this world fill men's souls, and leave no leisure for higher things. The bows were not given you only to shoot rabbits with for your own meals and your children's. They were given you to fight the good fight of faith with them.

The foundation of all is, that if we loved Jesus Christ

better, and were brought more closely into the fellowship of His love, and more under the dominion of the quickening, protective, and hallowing influences that flow from Him, we should not be able to help casting ourselves into the conflict which He has commanded, and in which He leads. Oh! brethren, if our faith were deeper, our love warmer, our devotion more ardent, our consecration more complete, our lives would be more befitting the lives of the soldiers of Jesus Christ.

If these things be the causes of the criminal dereliction of duty, the cures lie in the opposites of them. Especially we should seek to get and to keep nearer to Him for whom, if we fight at all, we shall fight; and by whom, if we conquer, we shall be victorious.

You remember the old story of the Scottish knight, with the king's heart in a golden casket, who, beset by crowds of dusky, turbaned believers, slung the precious casket into the serried ranks of the enemy, and with the shout, "Lead on, brave heart; I follow thee!" cast himself into the thickest of the fight, and lost his life that he might save it. And so, if we have Christ before us, we shall count no path too perilous that leads us to Him, but rather, hearing Him say, "If any man serve Me, let him follow Me," we shall walk in His footsteps, and fight the good fight, sustained by His example. And then, at the end, perhaps even we, all unworthy as we are, stained and imperfect as our poor service has been, may have the rapture of hearing from His lips the generous sentence which He once spoke in reference to an utterly useless gift, "She hath done what she could."

"AN INCREASING PURPOSE."

"AN INCREASING PURPOSE."

"These all, having had witness borne to them through their faith, received not the promise, God having provided some better thing concerning us, that they without us should not be made perfect."—HEB. xi. 39, 40 (R.V.).

IN their original application these words refer to the heroes of the faith whom the grand roll-call of this chapter has been enumerating. The whole company of Old Testament believers is included in "these all;" the whole company of New Testament believers in "us." The promise, the fulfilment of which they did not receive, was that of the Messiah and His salvation. They stretched out empty hands to greet it from afar, as sailors the dimly descried land, and possessed not that for which they longed, because God, looking onward through the ages, had mercifully willed that later generations should share in the blessing. The " better thing" foreseen, as given to us New Testament Christians, is the work of Christ, done at a point of time, but sending its influences backwards and forwards to bless all generations. The "perfecting" which it was not fitting that they should reach without us, is that final completeness in which all Christ's servants shall be united, and of which, since Christ has come, the saints of the older period have already received the earnest, as is manifest from their being subsequently spoken of as spirits "made perfect," and of which we too receive an earnest in another fashion, in the gift of the sanctifying Spirit.

Such being the original bearing of these words, we may venture to apply the principles contained in them in a somewhat different direction, as setting forth truths as to the relation of successive generations in the Church, all of whom have received that "better thing," which, given once for all in full completeness, is yet apprehended gradually by both individuals and the community, and blesses each generation of believing souls with new gifts of knowledge and power, till all are united in the ultimate perfection of the heavens. Our connection with the past, our task in the present, our anticipations in the future, are all taught in these great words.

I. We note, first, the bond uniting us with past generations.

"These all" had witness borne to them through their faith. That faith was their common characteristic, supplying a principle of unity which counterwrought the differences of era and circumstance, and made one company of persons so unlike as Abel and Rahab, Enoch and Jephthah. If we throw ourselves back to the condition of things at the date of this Epistle, this chapter appears even more remarkable than we usually consider it. The question then agitating men's minds was, Is not this new faith in Christ Jesus the destruction of Judaism? and the writer of this Epistle answers the question by the broad assertion that Christianity is the real Judaism, and that the true line of succession runs through the Church, and not through the synagogue. Fancy a stiff Pharisee's face at hearing a Christian teacher claim Abraham, Jacob, and, most audaciously of all, Moses for his side! But why did he do so? Because the foundation of their lives was faith. Their faith was the same. Their creeds were different, if not in essence, yet in comprehensiveness. Their faith was the same exercise of spirit as ours. Nay, the identity goes further still; for though faith in this Epistle be generally meant chiefly in its Old Testament sense of trust in God, and therefore in a future which is the subject of Divine promises, rather than in its New Testament specific sense of trust in Jesus, yet, since Jesus is the Revealer of God, its objects are substantially the same in both epochs of revelation. The secret of the religious life of the ancient believers is laid bare in one sentence concerning the father of them all: "Abraham believed God, and He counted it to him for righteousness." The object of their faith was God, as He spake at sundry times and in divers manners. The object of the Christian faith is God speaking in a Son, to listen to whom is to hear God, to see whom is to see the Father, and who is, as this Epistle elaborately proves, Priest and Temple and Sacrifice. The writer will not allow any difference, except that of development, between the call of prophet and psalmist, "Trust ye in the Lord for ever," and the preaching of apostles, "Believe on the Lord Jesus Christ." There has never been but one way to heaven, and faith has always been one, however different in completeness its creed.

It is but applying the same principle in a slightly different direction to say that all in Christian ages who have the same Spirit of faith are one. All who lay hold of the same Christ with the same confidence are knit together. But it must be the same Christ, the Divine-human Christ, the world's Redeemer; and the faith must be so far the same that it leans the whole weight of man's weakness on that incarnate Strength, and hangs all his hopes on that one Lord. If these things be the same, then no other differences, however great, can break the real unity, though, alas! they have often been permitted to break the consciousness of it. No matter in what age they lived, or what were their relations to one another, all holders of that faith, or rather all who are held by it, are one. Jewish converts with chips of the shell of Judaism still sticking to them, Egyptian hermits, African bishops, Donatist and orthodox, Latin monks, Lutheran professors, English Churchmen and Nonconformists, half-civilized converts in missionary stations—they all have the King's broad arrow on them. Faith is deepest, and they who are one in it are fundamentally one, however superficially separate. So, when we look back, there should be more than apathetic or curious glances, and more than the interest of the historian or controversialist. There should be the generous glow of kindred, and we should feel as we would by the graves of our ancestors. We should be aware of the tingle of the electric chain which binds in one all who hold by the one Lord; and however some narrow theories may part brethren from us, we should hold fast by the resolve that in heart at any rate we will not be parted from them, but in our sympathies strive to be true to the animating conviction that faith in Jesus Christ, the Saviour of the world, makes all its possessors one.

II. We note the better things foreseen for us.

There is no such advance within the limits of Christianity as separated it from the earlier revelation. The further "light" which each age has a right to expect is to "break forth from the Word" already given. "The Christ that is to be" is the Christ that was and is—"the same yesterday, and to-day, and for ever."

He is "for ever," as being complete. As for truth, all treasures of wisdom and knowledge are in Him, and may be drawn from the deepening understanding of the principles embodied in His life and death, in His resurrection and reign. All theology, morality, sociology, lie in Him as gold in ore, or diamonds in a matrix. As for powers, all that can be needed or done for the regeneration of the world and of single souls has been done and supplied in the work of Christ. What remains is but the application of the power which has been lodged in humanity. But while objective revelation is complete, and God's treasuries contain no "better thing" than the unspeakable gift once bestowed and ever possessed, there is meant to be advancement in understanding of the truth and in appropriation of the power. Jesus is inexhaustible. No one man can absorb Him all; no one age can. A thousand mirrors set round that central light will each receive its beam at its own angle, and flash it back in its own fashion. So true progress will consist in a fuller understanding and firmer grasp of Him as Son of God and Redeemer of the world, and in a more complete reception of His Spirit, manifested in more Christ-like characters and more Christ-pleasing service. It does not mean casting away the old, but finding new force in the old commandment and new depth of meaning in the old revelation. In this alphabet, alpha is omega, and both Alpha and Omega are Christ. Each generation, then, has to receive an incomplete work from its predecessors, and to hand on an incomplete work, made a little less incomplete by its faithful diligence, to its successors. The great cathedral took centuries to rear, and each generation had but to raise its walls a yard or two, and a man might be glad if it were granted him to add some fair carving to a single shaft, or to lay but a single stone.

But within these limits there is room for large advance, and in periods of swift change like ours, it is hard to estimate gains and losses as between the new and the old. Temperament and age will affect our sympathies and make our appreciation partial, and it is a piece of very pressing Christian duty for each of us to see that we do not let the "personal equation" so influence us as to make us either the sanguine and exclusive eulogists of the new, or the pessimistic and obstinate partisans of the old. We may not be better than our fathers, but we have some better thing than they had, for which we have to thank God. We have gained inasmuch as theology has become more Christ-centred. The Gospels are more to the Church of to-day than they ever were before. There is less of mere doctrine, and more of Jesus Christ. His present activity as Lord of the universe and King of men is increasingly set forth, and the good news of God is being disembarrassed of misty metaphysics which were once thought to be theology. The interminable controversy between the bare conception of an omnipotent will, and the equally crude one of a free human will, has ceased to interest. The love of God stands where for many generations the will of God was set—in the centre. The progressive character of revelation has become an article of belief, and has made the Bible a new book, throbbing with life on all its pages. Christianity has become more sympathetic, and begins to recognize its duty as to social questions. The missionary task of the Church has been accepted by all Churches which have any life in them, and of late years we have seen wonderful increase of personal service by all sorts of Christian people. Nor should we overlook, in our summing up of the good in this our day, the sharpened interest in religious questions, so characteristic of it, even though that interest is often hostile to the claims of Christ. We should share the confidence of the brave apostle, who counted " many adversaries " as the sign of "a great door and effectual," and a reason for protracting his stay in so hopeful a field.

But every better may become a worse. If former generations grasped too exclusively the conception of the sovereign Divine will, they were made strong men thereby. If their religion was too largely dogmatic theology, they thereby won intense convictions, and a familiarity with profound and ennobling thoughts, which saved life from triviality, and devotion from degenerating into mere emotion. If their morality was somewhat rigid and stern, it kept them grave and pure. If they were too much secluded from the currents of literature, art, and science, their souls were focussed on one thing, and the concentrated light burned. Their narrowness meant depth, and if a stream is to be wholesome, which it can only be by movement, depth is better than a breadth which too often is possible only through shallowness.

They had the defects of their qualities. So have we. There is danger that definite doctrinal belief and teaching shall be diminished to the vanishing point, partly from the infection of the unreasonable revolt against " theology," and partly from the influence of evangelistic fervour, which asks for " the simple gospel." There is danger of so presenting the love of God as to neutralize His righteousness and His wrath, thereby losing the mighty power for persuading men which lies in knowing the terror of the Lord.

There is danger of obscuring the characteristic of the gospel as good news of redemption, and of the pulpit's becoming a professor's desk or a social reformer's platform. We have said that all social and ethical truth is involved in and to be deduced from the facts of Christ's nature and mission, but the first aspect of these facts is their power to bring forgiveness and peace to guilty consciences. Our wisdom and our success will be to keep to the Divine order, and ever make the first and prominent characteristic of the gospel, which we believe and hold forth, its power to deliver the single soul from its burden of sin, through faith in the sacrifice of Jesus Christ, and then to set forth its power to furnish the bases of all individual and social action, in the ethics that are enwrapped in its glad tidings that "God so loved the world, that He gave His only begotten Son, that whosoever believeth in Him should not perish." We hear much now of applied Christianity and of the social mission of the gospel. Let us not forget that there must be individual Christianity before there can be social, and that it must be possessed before it can be applied, and that the personal faith of sinful men in Jesus Christ's work as their personal Saviour is the beginning of all.

There are dangers, too, arising from changed conditions of life. Wealth has brought secularity in its train. Education has introduced familiarity with un-Christian and anti-Christian works of genius and learning. Public and political life has opened a more attractive arena for those who in other days would have found their work in more distinctively religious service. The whirl of modern life in which religious people are caught up has diminished habits of quiet meditation and devotion. Even the awakened sense of responsibility for the neglected, and the consequent abundance of work and of workers, bring snares. On the whole, it may well be questioned whether the modern types of religion have not lost much that it would have been gain to keep, and gained something that it would have been better to have lost. Is not personal religion at a low ebb? Have we not lost much of the depth and unworldliness of ancient piety? Where are the ancient intense realization of unseen realities, the ardour of communion, the continual sense of a Divine presence, the atmosphere of separation surrounding the Christian heart? The change from old days is not all progress. We need the exhortation, unwelcome as it is in the ears of an epoch which is so proud of its gains in mechanical arts and physical sciences that it has made contempt of the past into an article of its creed, "Remember the days of old, consider the years of many generations: ask thy father, and he will show thee; thine elders, and they will tell thee."

Let us beware lest we let go the precious with the vile, and, while we fancy ourselves far ahead of the "simple and narrow" religion of the past, should really be casting away the very essence of revealed Christianity, and with it the depth and fervour of personal godliness, in grasping at the impossible phantom of a religion in harmony with that kind of "modern thought" which will not tolerate the supernatural, nor bow before the Christ who is the Son of God and the Redeemer of the world. If these two fundamental truths are falteringly held, we shall soon have to cry, "Where be all His miracles which our fathers told us of?" But if to the good things which past ages discovered in these, we add the better things which God, by the march of events and the evolution of new powers in the old gospel to deal with new problems of this eager day so full of possibilities and promise even in its antagonisms, is bestowing on the Churches, if they are wise and large-hearted enough to welcome and accept them, then the former days will not be better than these; but this age too shall be able to reproduce and transcend the triumphs of the past, and shall acknowledge with thankful wonder, "As we have heard, so have we seen in the city of the Lord of hosts, in the city of our God."

III. The yet better things in reserve for our successors.

Naturally the progress is not to stop with us, but will go on as long as there is a Church on earth. We, too, have but partial light, and have partially appropriated the gifts and discharged the duties given and enjoined in the partly understood gospel. How much has yet to be done before all the truth as it is in Jesus is drawn out into the consciousness of Christians and incorporated in their lives! How much more before it passes from the Church to the world, and transforms it into a Church! No doubt future generations will look back on our insensibility to the flagrant contradictions of the social ethics of Christianity, which they will, no doubt, discern in our lives, with the same kind of half-pitying, half-amused condemnation with which we look back on "ages of faith," which were ages of cruelty, ignorance, and persecution, or with which we discover that the devout author of the great treatise on the " Freedom of the Will" was a devout slaveholder. Slavery is now recognized as unchristian. War is beginning to be so. What venerable institution which the Churches have canonized will the keener insight of our successors expel from the place of honour? The Church of the future will have broken down all sects. Religion will one day be harmonized with "science." Christian principles will be applied to social and national life with revolutionary effects. Many of the evils are already like ringed trees in Australian forests, forbidden at all events to expand, and sure in time to die. There will be a fuller baptism of the Spirit on the happier Church that is to be, resulting in more consecrated lives, in more missionary and evangelistic effort, and in a finer harmony of nature and a more symmetrical and majestic development of capacities in the individual and the community. Much destructive work will have to be done before that consummation is reached. Does any man suppose that the existing embodiments of Christianity, the churches of this day, are meant to be permanent?

Let us not fear. There is a trembling for the ark of God, which is the fitting issue of the trembler's consciousness of his own unfaithful service. But the ark is safe, whatever may become of the cart that bears it, or the oxen that draw it. Out of the wild sea of tossing contraries of opinion will rise a shape of fairer beauty than hitherto has blessed the earth, like the moon swimming up serene and large from some unquiet ocean. Not one grain of the true wheat shall fall to the ground, though a million Satans had the Churches to sift. There is an exaggerated conservatism which does not love the old so much as it hates the new, and which understands neither. The men who stoned Stephen for the sake of Moses would have stoned Moses for the sake of Abraham. The things that can be shaken will be removed, that the things which cannot be shaken may remain; as some great building, round whose sides have clustered paltry sheds that hid its fair proportions with their obtrusive meanness, stands out the fairer when they are swept away. The central truth of the Divinity and sacrifice of the Christ of God is the imperishable core of the Christian faith. These and the related necessarily involved truths being preserved, everything is preserved; for these truths, wielded by the Spirit dwelling in the Church, have power to weave their own vestures, and will in every age mould the forms of Christian thought and life into such shapes as may best correspond to the wants of each age, and most completely subserve the increasing purpose which runs through all the ages, and which each age is honoured by helping forward towards realization.

IV. Our text necessarily includes the idea of the final perfecting in which all are united.

The saints of the old and the believers of the new covenant are not to be perfected apart. A blessed future union is shadowed in the words, as it is required by the whole scope of the considerations suggested to us by them.

There is to be a perfect union of all in the common joy of possession of the common gift. On the march the pilgrims were widely separated, but in the camp their tents will be near each other. All who follow the one Shepherd shall be one flock. We can say nothing of the manner of that wondrous future union, which baffles our grasp when we think of the multitudes of whom the flock is composed. But just as Dante saw Paradise under the symbol of a great rose, whose many petals were yet one flower, and just as astronomers tell us that the giant nebulæ, consisting of infinite numbers of suns, are yet each one whole, though we cannot imagine what forces bind together across such bewildering spaces, so all who in solitude here, and amid misconceptions and diversities, have yet loved the one Lord and followed the one Shepherd, shall couch round Him above, and in some mysterious but most blessed manner know that they "live together" and all "together with Him," as the bond of their unity, and perhaps the medium of their intercourse. There will be a united perfecting in the common possession of the whole Christ. Even then star will differ from star, and we may venture to believe that each will share his special refraction of the central light with others, and the beams of the variously coloured stars lovingly blend in perfect whiteness. "Neither said any among them that any of the things which he possessed was his own, but they had all things common."

There will be united perfection in enjoying the results of the long unfolding through the ages of the fulness of Christ. Here one generation originates and another completes. It is given to few to see the triumph of the cause for which they have fought, or the successful working of the plans which they have inaugurated. "One soweth, and another reapeth," is the law for earth. But the time comes when all the workers shall share in the gladness of the finished work; when all who, separated by long ages, and thick walls of mutual misconception and divergence in practice and opinion, have yet been unknowingly toiling towards the same end, shall clasp inseparable hands in the great result which contains all their work. Division of labour is multiplication of joy and reward. The sower cannot go into the waving harvest and pick out the ears which have sprung from the seed which he sowed. The reaper cannot go up to the stack and identify the sheaves that fell before his sickle. The brook cannot recover its drops from the mighty river or the all-enclosing ocean. But the one great result shall gladden all who have ever helped to bring it, and the sower who went forth in sadness shall come back, bearing "the sheaves" that are his, though another reaped them.

So, then, friends, let us set ourselves to our small tasks, happy if we can push forward by the least space the boundary of Christ's kingdom, or absorb and reflect a sparkle of His light. Let us be reverent of those who have gone before, and thankful for that which they have handed down to us. Let us pass it on, mended and increased by our toil, to those who shall catch up our dropped torches and complete our unfinished work. And, above all, let us take as the end of these thoughts that stirring exhortation to which our text leads up: "Wherefore seeing we also are compassed about with so great a cloud of witnesses, let us lay aside every weight, and the sin which doth so easily beset us, and let us run with patience the race that is set before us, looking unto Jesus," in whom every age finds its Leader, and all the generations of His saints shall at last find their common heaven of perfection.

THE DEFENCE OF THE DEFENCELESS.

THE DEFENCE OF THE DEFENCELESS.

"A land of unwalled villages . . . them that are at rest, that dwell safely, all of them dwelling without walls, and having neither bars nor gates."—EZEK. xxxviii. 11.

"Jerusalem shall be inhabited as towns without walls. . . . For I, saith the Lord, will be unto her a wall of fire round about, and will be the glory in the midst of her."—ZECH. ii. 4, 5.

I HAVE taken these two passages together because the language in the latter is evidently the echo of that in the former. In both, we have the description of a community dwelling in a fashion very unusual, and very risky in old times, namely, in the open country, without any walls, bars, or gates to their cities.

But in the former passage these dwellers in the open are represented as becoming, by reason of their defenceless and fancied security, the prey of a cruel conqueror, who comes to "take them for a spoil;" whereas in the latter text, people living in precisely the same fashion, without walls, bars, or bolts, are represented as being in absolute security—"because I, saith the Lord, will be a wall of fire round about them, and a glory in the midst of them." That is to say, there are two kinds of carelessness in the world, two kinds of security and supposed safety; the one foolish and fatal, the other devout and good. We may be dwelling like fools in unwalled cities, when all the land around us is laid waste by enemies; or we may be dwelling like wise men in unwalled cities, because there is a flaming barrier between us and evil, through which nothing that harms can ever come.

And these two conditions, to the eye of sense, will look very much the same; but, to an eye that sees deeper, will be as different as heaven is from hell. We have brought out, then, by the juxtaposition of these two passages, with their identities and differences, the vivid contrast between these two ways of life, and the tragic unlikeness of their respective ends.

I. The first text presents an instance of a defenceless security which is blind presumption.

In old times the first condition of dwelling safely was to find either a site which was inaccessible, or to surround the city with a wall which was impregnable.

All old cities are usually perched upon hill-tops, or are surrounded by walls, which, in these "piping times of peace," are generally being turned into boulevards and gardens. Cities that trusted to anything except strong natural or artificial fortifications, sooner or later became the prey of the enemy. So the phrases of these texts, which are found in Ezekiel, and caught up by Zechariah, appear once or twice besides in Scripture, describing the condition of exceptional communities—in one case far away in the desert, and in another, hidden in an almost inaccessible corner between the spurs of the Lebanon, where the men of Dan, as it is said, dwelt quiet and secure, far from any men, and having no business with any.

Such defencelessness was unwise, augured rashness, and

was likely to lead to disaster. Is the temper of security in which so many of us live less absurd or dangerous?

An extraordinary access of foolhardiness seems to dominate the lives of the mass of men, which leads them to neglect the plainest facts, and run risks that can only be called tremendous. Every life has possible and certain dangers, against which it is surely the part of common sense to provide. A wise man will look ahead, and make sure, before they come, that he has some protection against them. Death will come; changes and losses will come. The strongest props will be taken away, the closest embrace unclasped; hearts will be torn apart, and the one which bleeds to death be happier than its companion which feebly throbs and keenly aches alone. Strength will decay, disappointments will fret, and failures depress the powers. Sickness, solitude, pecuniary losses, abortive schemes, prodigal sons, and a thousand other ills, are either certain or possible. These are the heavy-armed battalions of the foe; and besides them, there are swarms of more lightly accoutred skirmishers—like gnats from a bog—sure to harass, and making up in numbers what they want in weight.

And, for the most part, calamities come suddenly. Sometimes, indeed, there is the slow gathering of the livid thunderclouds, and an awful brooding pause before the crash. But generally evils come with little warning, however long they stay. How many lives we have all known shattered for all their remaining years by a bolt from the blue! One sudden blow, the unheralded work of a moment, puts an apparent eternity between the moment before it and that after it. No day dawns on earth without rising on some happy, careless, and secure, on whom it sets, desolate, ruined, crushed; and no man knows, when he wakes in the morning, but that he may be rising to meet the blackest day of his life; unless, indeed, he may have already drunk the bitterest draught that Fortune can compound, and so have a kind of sad immunity, as having outlived the worst, and bought security by the loss of his dearest treasure. We are like the inhabitants of a winding glen, the curves of which hide the enemy till he bursts, with fire and sword, on the undefended huts. We know not what may be just ready to rush on us at the next turning.

Seeing, then, that so many evils must come, and so many may come, and that both the certain and the uncertain are likely to break on us without warning, how unaccountable and incredible, if it were not so universal, is the habit of living quite comfortably without any defence against these! There is nothing stranger in all the strange vagaries and irrationalities of men, than their way of blinding themselves to unwelcome certainties and probabilities. Most men are impatient of serious reflection on the realities of their position, and the indisposition is fostered by the continual demands of the moment, and the necessity for prompt attention to them. We possess, and are foolish enough to exercise, that strange power of ignoring disagreeable things, however certain. It is difficult, too, to realize in thought a condition unlike the present, or to make vivid and operative on conduct the picture of one's self when deprived of some familiar and long-enjoyed good. "To-morrow shall be as this day, and much more abundant," is the natural language of unreflecting levity. It is not only the "sluggard" who might profitably go to school to an ant-hill. The improvident man, who will not believe that winter is coming, while the land is yellow with autumn sheaves, may well "consider her ways," and, like her, "gather food in harvest" for the certainly dark and cold days that are at hand. Many of us are like the peasants who build their houses and plant their vineyards on the slopes of Vesuvius, and live light-heartedly, ignoring the possible future, though in the day the thin column of ominous smoke whitens a thin strip of ominous blue sky, and in the night the dull red of the lava tinges the sides of the cone. Some day there must be, and any day there may be, an outburst, and grey ashes will cover the vines, and earthquake crack the walls of the houses, and ruin and haply death fall upon the careless tenants. They run all risks, and manage somehow to banish thoughts of the risks which they run. So do thousands of us in regard to far graver perils, far more certain to assail us and more disastrous in their destructiveness. Whole battalions of them threaten us all. We may make "conditions of peace" with them, if by prudent foresight and appropriate precautions we "send an embasage" while they are at a distance; for evils foreseen and prepared for are robbed of much of their power to hurt, in losing their power to surprise. We may even make them our friends if we take them aright, which we are much more likely to do if we have anticipated their coming and rehearsed them beforehand. Come they will, and if they find us unprepared, their blow will be stunning and may be fatal.

Nor is it only the usual refusal to contemplate these lowering certainties and possibilities beforehand which leaves us defenceless. Another phase of favourite folly is the conceit of our power to cope with the enemy when he comes. "Unwalled villages" are tokens of an overweening confidence in the strong arms of the villagers, which will be rudely shattered some day. How can a man front his probable and certain future, and keep his sanity, if he have not God for his Defence? One is tempted to say that he can only do it because he has not sense enough to go mad. If we had clearly before us the reality, in its true colour, form, magnitude, pressure, and duration, who of us could venture to say, "Alone I can meet it and endure"? But, partly because we ignore the unwelcome, partly because our power of forecast is mercifully limited, lest future bitterness should poison present sweetness, partly because that too feeble realization of impending disaster enables us to cheat ourselves into believing that we can cope with it when it falls, we go on, comfortably enough, in our "unwalled villages," without bars or bolts, and seldom think of the sudden foe who may burst into the quiet seclusion of the unguarded valley. Like the people of Dan, to whom one of our texts refers, we may dwell "quiet and secure," in the proper meaning of that word—without care—though, alas! to be without care is not to be without peril, and to be "secure" is a very different thing from being "safe." The original reads in our first text, "them that are at rest, that dwell securely," or confidently, and thereby expresses not the reality of the villagers' condition, but the foolhardy illusions of their imaginations, which were so soon to be shattered by the invader bursting in "to take the spoil and to take the prey."

So, sooner or later, comes the crash, as the context of our first text tells us. The destroyer is attracted by the defencelessness of the self-confident villagers, and they fall an easy prey. The less the preparation and defence, the more bitter the defeat and destruction. Surely, then, it is madness to carry on full sail till a typhoon strikes the ship. It is no time then to be hauling down sails and battening down hatches. If we do not prepare for the storm, and prefer not to look at the sinking barometer, we shall probably founder while we are trying to do what could have been easily done before. When the enemy is blowing his trumpets for the assault just outside the village, it is too late to begin drawing plans of fortifications, or hurrying with spades and barrows to fling up earthworks. It is no doubt well not to be "over-exquisite to cast the fashion of uncertain evils," but not to look certain ones in the face, nor have any notion beforehand of what we propose to do when they come, as come they will, is simple insanity, and would be recognized as such, if the bulk of men did not keep each other in countenance in committing it. This is no world for unwalled villages. Flesh is too sensitive and swords too sharp to allow of wisely dwelling in such. The "quiet" of the men who do so will be terribly disturbed. Their defenceless security is blind presumption.

II. Our second text brings out, in strong contrast to the former, a security which is externally like it, but really opposed to it, namely, the security of quiet faith.

The two states of mind are apparently identical, just as the ideal Jerusalem of Zechariah's vision looked exactly like these other unwalled towns. The prophecy was not fulfilled in the real, rebuilt Jerusalem; but the prophet's eye saw the ideal city, extending beyond the rocky peninsula, to which the real one was confined, and stretching far on every side, like some of the great cities which the exiles had learned to know, containing wide pastures and much cattle, and looking like an assemblage of villages, each among its fields and groves. But the ideal Jerusalem is to have no walls as Babylon had, and to be safer without than Babylon was with these. One thing made the difference between the unwalled Jerusalem, in which dwelling is safe, and the unwalled villages which seemed like it, and dwelling in which is ruinous. The reason why Jerusalem has no walls is, "For I, saith the Lord, will be unto her a wall of fire round about, and I will be the glory in the midst of her." A fiery bulwark around, a flaming glory within, belong to her, and make other walls ludicrous superfluities. The presence of Jehovah is at once defence and illumination. That flaming fire is everywhere at once, around and within. At one and the same time it burns threateningly between the city and her foes, and shines lambently, a light in every dwelling; "and the city hath no need of the sun, neither of the moon to shine upon it, for the glory of God did lighten it." Therefore it is safe to have no other walls.

Take the truth conveyed in this grand vision, laying aside metaphor, and it is this: The very same temper which without God is insanity, with God is simple duty, high privilege, and the supremest wisdom. "Take no thought for the morrow." He that has not God to take thought for him, and puts that exhortation in practice, will wreck his life. "I would have you without carefulness." A man that has no "carefulness" for himself, and yet has not cast all his anxiety upon God, who takes an interest in him and undertakes for him, will soon have cause to repent his recklessness. "To-morrow shall be as this day, and much more abundant." The drunkard says that in the original use of the phrase. The saint says it too. The former is wrong and foolish for saying it; the other says it, and is as sure that it is so as that there is a God in heaven.

So the very same temper of careless security, which in a godless man wrecks and ruins both heart and life, in a Christian man is highest joy and clearest wisdom. For the all-important difference between the two is that round one of them there is, and round the other there is not, the strong defence of an Almighty protection; and in the heart of the man that thus has cast himself upon God, and not in the other, there burns, beneficent and illuminating, the unflickering flame of a Divine glory.

"A wall of fire round about us." Yes! but if it is to be outside us, to defend, it must first be within us, to enlighten and make us glad. And if thus guarded by, and thus filled with, the Divine light, which is at once purity and gladness and knowledge, we cast all our care upon Him, it is not folly to say, "I need no bulwarks, no towers along the steep. The Lord is my Defence, because the Holy One of Israel is my King."

Of course we are not to suppose that such words as those of my second text forbid the use of common sense, diligence, and effort in providing for the inevitable future, in so far as these can help to provide for it. Zechariah prophesied that the Jerusalem which he saw should have no walls. But Zechariah was one of the men who helped to build the walls of the real Jerusalem, whose restoration was largely owing to him. In like manner, we are not forbidden, by the requirements of Christian resignation and faith in God, to forsake any precautions which common prudence—which, in fact, is His voice—suggests to us to take. But we are forbidden to fancy that these are our defences and security. Use them, and yet look beyond them to Him who alone can give the blessing.

Now, all that I have been saying may be gathered into two words. How foolish it is to front life and what it may bring, and death and what it must bring, without God for our Defence! And how yet more foolish, if that be possible, it is for those who have God for their Defence to be troubled and careful about many things, or anything! "We have a strong city; salvation will God appoint for walls and bulwarks." Let us keep behind them, and trust in no arm of flesh, but in the unseen defence of the ever-present God; and let us seek first to have Him for a glory in the midst of us, and then surely He will be a wall of fire round about us.

HOW A CHURCH LIVES AND GROWS.

HOW A CHURCH LIVES AND GROWS.

"From whom the whole body, by joints and bands having nourishment ministered and knit together, increaseth with the increase of God."—Col. ii. 19.

It may assist us to grasp more clearly the fulness of thought in these words if we disentangle the main idea from the subsidiary clauses gathered round it. That main thought is that from Christ, the Head, the whole body increases. Three things are contained therein—the source of the life, the derived growth, the oneness of the body and the participation of all its parts in that growth. But this main thought is enriched and arabesqued, as it were, in Paul's eager, impetuous fashion, with pregnant additions. He seldom draws a plain straight line, but surrounds it with many a curve and involution, like the light, flower-like decorations which encrust the firm framework of the upper spire of Antwerp Cathedral. They hide but do not weaken the direct upward spring of the rigid metal. His thoughts come fast and press on one another, and the result seems, to careless readers, confusion, when it is but the prodigality of a fertile soil quickened by the warmth of Christ's love into productiveness, which is richness, not riot.

The subsidiary clause describes more fully the twofold manner of the growth of the body, and the office in relation to that growth, of the subordinate parts. The body is a whole, made up of parts differing, and therefore adapted and harmonious. These have each their function in transmitting the life. That life manifests itself in the double effect of assimilating nourishment and effecting compaction. There are, then, large truths involved in this representation, as to the source of vitality, the various and harmonious action of all the parts, the consequent growth of the whole, and the individual union to Christ, which is the condition of all individual and corporate increase which is healthy and according to God.

I. We have to consider the Source of all the life of the body.

According to the context, Christ is the Head, and, as Paul puts it without being very careful about physiological accuracy, therefore the source from which all parts of the body partake of a common life. There are three symbols chiefly employed to represent the union of Christ with His Church, one of them being that used by Christ Himself, and the others principally by Paul. One knows not which presents that real and mysterious bond in the most striking fashion. These are the emblems of the vine, the body, and the marriage bond—the first drawn from the noblest example of plant life as conceived by the old world; the second, from the noblest type of animal existence; and the third, from the deepest and closest union of human spirits. The first expresses the calm, effortless, uninterrupted process by which the sap rises in the branches and broadens in the leaves, and loads the boughs with purple clusters. The repetition of similar parts is the characteristic of vegetable growth. The second brings into view more of the notion of exercise and office on the part of the limbs of the body, which do not grow without effort, and may be diseased and disabled. Variety of parts co-operating in one growing whole is the characteristic of animal increase. The third lifts our thoughts into the region of love and voluntary choice, and reminds us of the original distinctness of the persons who become one, because they love and therefore wish to be one. When we look up into some great tree, which to our northern eyes is a nobler type of vegetable growth than a vine, and mark the clouds of foliage, and measure how far it is from the firm bole and the deep roots to the tiny leaflet at the topmost tip of the furthest branch, we gain a wonderful image of the unity of life which permeates the Church. But still more expressive of the deep mystery which is involved in the thought of the oneness of Christ and His people is that other symbol of the body and its head. The mystery is part of the felicity of the figure. Who can explain the connection of soul and body, the process by which the thrill of a nerve becomes emotion, and the throb of a bit of grey matter in the skull a thought? Who can tell us what life is? Verbal definitions are plentiful enough, but they help little to the comprehension of the thing. That commonest of facts, which makes dead matter glow and move under spiritual stress, is still inexplicable after anatomist's scalpels and pyschologist's abstractions have done their best to lay bare its secret. Of man in his complex nature we may reverently say, as we say of God, in whose image he is made in regard to part of his being, "clouds and darkness are round about him." We may expect no less thick darkness to rest upon that mysterious and blessed union which makes the dust and ashes of sinful humanity into a living body, glowing and moulded by the spirit of life which was in Christ. We can get no deeper down nor further back than His own claim, "I am the Life."

But that union, though mysterious, is most real. It is not merely that Jesus Christ gives to those who trust and obey Him certain gifts as from without, which gifts may be possessed and retained in the absence of the Giver, but that He is in His people individually and collectively, and by His indwelling imparts life within. What keeps a body from becoming a carcase? The life. What keeps a Church from becoming an offence and a stench? Christ, who is the Head to the body, His Church, and more than the head is to the physical body, since He is not only the sovereign Member but the all-pervading Life, whose seat is not in this gland or that part of the brain, but everywhere, filling all, and quickening each part of the mighty whole with the capacity for reception and the power of action proper to it.

II. Note the various and harmonious action of all the parts.

We need not inquire particularly as to the physiological doctrines underlying the metaphor of the text, or seek for the precise equivalents in the social organization of the Church for the "joints and bands" referred to. It is enough for our purpose to note the twofold office which these discharge. They receive from the Head and communicate to the body the double gifts of nutrition and unity. They originate nothing, but all which they impart they first derive from Him. However it may be in the physical body, in the spiritual analogue which is the community of Christian souls, each member has both the direct communication of life and its gifts from the Head, even Christ, and the indirect participation by means of gifts received through the brotherly mediation of others. He who has no personal access to the fountain of life, nor ever draws at first hand from it, will profit little by anything that men can say or do for him; but, on the other hand, he who does not value and use the gifts bestowed at first on his brethren that they may filter to others, will be apt to have a disproportioned development of the life, and often to mistake his own imaginations for Christ's voice, and his own inclinations for Christ's command. Exaggerated individualism on the one side, and dependence on the reports of Christ's mind and will brought by others on the other, are equally far from the type of character which corresponds to the two facts in question, namely, that the life which the Head imparts to His Church is imparted both by direct contact of the individual soul with its Lord, and through the medium of other members of the body. The direct communication between Jesus and the soul does not make the help of brethren superfluous. The agency of human teachers and guides or of the collective body, does not supersede the need for the direct contact of each soul with Christ. "Joints and bands" minister nutriment and compaction, but only on condition that they are fed from the true bread of life, partaken of by that faith which is the personal contact of the single soul with the sole Redeemer, and are knit to all who hold the Head, because they realize their own union to Him by their own grasp. The linked chain clasp hands and thus transmit the thrill from Him, but each unit in the chain grasps the Lord's hand with his own, or no tingle of influence will reach him through his fellows.

From Jesus comes all nourishment of the Divine life,

even when we think that we instruct or stimulate each other. He is the Fountain of wisdom and good, and whatever may be the vessels which bring the water to our lips, they are filled by Him and with Him. Just as the bread which we earn by the sweat of our own brows, or receive by the hospitality of others, comes in truth from a Divine hand opened to supply the wants of every living thing, so, but in still more wonderful all-pervasiveness of influence, does Jesus feed all souls with the Bread which is Himself.

From Jesus comes the oneness of the body. Many attempts have been made to secure that unity in other ways, and to knit other bonds than His own all-present and compacting life; but these are vain, substituting mechanical and formal for real oneness. Agreement in opinions as expressed by creeds, uniformity of polity as crystallized in organizations or forms of worship, and the like, are but poor travesties of the one true principle of unity. The oneness of the branches of the vine, in which the same life manifests itself in wood and leaf and cluster, is not more unlike the artificial oneness of a bundle of faggots held together by a piece of string, than is the true oneness of the true Church of Christ to that of these artificial agglomerations. The one derived life is the only real bond of unity. In the old covenant, the seven-branched candlestick represented the formal unity of Israel, which was one by reason of mere natural descent from one ancestor, and the rigid stiffness of the symbol may be taken as expressive of the mechanical and external nature of the bond which held the tribes together. But the golden candlestick lies deep in the sea, and in the new covenant order its place is taken by the seven which the seer beheld, which are one in their sevenfoldness because the ascended Lord walks in the midst of them. This is a better unity than that of old. The nearer, then, we draw to Jesus Christ, the nearer we shall be to one another. The radii of a circle are closer together the closer they are to the centre, and if we who stand round Jesus Christ travel each on our own direct line of progress towards Him, we shall find ourselves in closer neighbourhood with separated brethren journeying to the one point to which widely removed and even opposite paths converge. Life, and life alone, resists the chemical and other forces which tend to disintegrate the physical body. Death means resolving that into its elements. Union to Jesus Christ is the bond and the power of true unity.

Since these issues of the Divine life are ministered by the members, even while all derived from the Head, we may lay to heart the manifold uses of fellowship and the need which each has of others. The true value of Church union is much obscured to-day, not only by the many other forms of association which fill so large a place in modern life, but also by the opposite and mutually producing exaggerations of theories in which the Church is everything and the individual nothing, and of those in which individualism is so asserted that there is scant justice done to the idea of the community. It is hard to keep the true path between these extremes. But if we give due weight to the two short clauses of this text, "from whom" on the one hand, and "by joints and bands" on the other, we shall at least have the materials for a duly proportioned estimate of the two modes of thought, which are complementary and harmonious, though often pitted against each other.

It is not good for man to be alone, and the religious life which is developed in solitary reliance on the individual perception of truth in Christ and reception of grace from Him will usually be deformed by exaggeration of individual peculiarities, and disproportioned prominence given to fragments of truth. It is not good for man to be so lost in the community as to distrust his own judgment, enlightened by the Spirit of Christ, unless he has its sentences endorsed by the body, or to depend only on other men and on rites for spiritual supplies. "From Christ" relegates the soul in the last resort to Jesus as the Source of all its life and nourishment; "by joints and bands" bids it thankfully use brotherly mediation.

Since the laws of nourishment and growth are thus stated, each member of the whole body has its work. In these offices there is the greatest variety, just as there are many organs with different functions in the physical body. The same life is light in the eye, strength in the arm, colour in the cheek, music on the tongue, swiftness in the foot. "So also is Christ." The higher we rise in the scale of being, the more the organs are differentiated, and each confined to its special function. The lowest form of life is but a sac, which can be turned inside out without harm, and has no division of labour to separate portions of the unspecialized whole. So in society, the more it is developed, the more are its members confined to ever narrower ranges of work. In primitive communities, each man does all the simple offices which any man does. The measure of "civilization" is the limitation of function. So in the Church, the effect of Christianity is to develop individual character, and also to knit men more closely together. The whole octave is needed. Diversity is the condition of harmony.

Do we not, then, fail in tolerance? We are all apt to

require that all voices shall sing our part, forgetting that the whole score must be sounded in order to represent the great master's purpose. We fail in welcoming different modes of work, different reproductions of the perfect life, different reflections and refractions of the light. We fail in courage to be ourselves, to see for ourselves and to act accordingly, one after this manner and one after that. White light is produced by the blending of all rays of different hue. It needs the combination of all types of excellence and of all partial glimpses of truth to set forth the fulness of that Christ who filleth all in all, and is more than all. "All these worketh that one and the selfsame Spirit, dividing to every man severally as He will." Let us, then, take heed that we are good stewards of the manifold grace of God, honouring its variety of operations in the Christians most unlike ourselves, and cultivating the special form of its gifts entrusted to us, neither trying to make others like ourselves nor ourselves like others.

III. Note the consequent increase of the whole.

"The increase of God" is a solemn expression, which may either refer to the increase of the Divine life in the members of the body, or to the increase of the body from without. Probably both ideas were in the apostle's mind. He would have us discriminate between other sorts of growth and that only wholesome kind, of which God is the Author, which is imparted from Christ to those who, as the previous verse describes, "hold the Head."

The increase of life in the Church, then, both as a community and in its separate elements, depends on the harmonious activity of all the parts. Not only does each organ contribute to health and growth, but the condition of its own health and growth is its activity. The disused member atrophies. The used faculty is strengthened. "To him that hath shall be given." If a man in Christ desires His own religious character to be deepened, let him exercise the religion he has, and by it control his life. Let it underlie his actions, and let him translate all his creed into conduct, and set all his devout emotions to drive the wheels of daily duty. Faith exercised will become more clear and long-sighted, like the sailor's keen eyes, and will see the land that is very far off, where others are aware of nothing but cloud. The true way to increase any Christ-like trait of character is to give it full scope in life.

The collective growth in the Divine life is also dependent on the activity of all, and sadly hampered when some are idle. A very insignificant member of the physical frame can become of immense importance by failing to do its work, and there are many professing Christians who are able by the same method to stop much progress. The dead weight of carelessness and non-participation in Christian life and service which every Church has to carry terribly retards its progress. A tiny clot of blood blocking a thread-like artery can kill a man. The inert masses of nominal Christians have arrested the march of every outburst of quickened religious life, as we hear of armies of caterpillars stopping trains. So much heat has to be expended in converting ice into water, that there is little left for making the water boil and give steam. We have all more power to help than we often believe, and far more to hinder than we think.

In like manner the increase of the Church from without depends on its vitality within, and on the concurrent activity of all its members. The great Lord of the household has left "to every man his work," and no one can neglect his own task without damaging the well-being of the household. Great gifts designate for great work, as it is called by vulgar opinion; but great or small are adjectives which have no place in God's judgment of our service. The smallest part of a machine is as needful as the largest for the working of the machine. Ignorant spectators admire the huge cranks and polished columns of steel which serve as pistons; but take away a screw or two half an inch long and unseen, and crank and piston are motionless. The feeble members, says Paul, are necessary. Great and small, weak and strong, are man's adjectives, often wrongly applied and always foreign to the Divine criterion of work, which is not its magnitude, but its motive and its aim.

But the increase of the body from without depends not only on the action of all its parts, but on their health and vitality. Work for Christ is warranted and efficacious only when it is a consequence of life in Christ. There must first be life, and then the acts of life. And this sequence is needful to be kept steadily in view in these busy days, when so many voices urge to activity. It has come to be the fashion to engage in some kind of Christian service, and, amid all this bustle, there is danger that the inward communion, without which all the outward service lacks its consecration and its power, may be starved. The galvanized twitchings of a corpse simulate life's movements in a ghastly parody; and much of the whipped-up activity of Christian people, to which so many voices urge now, is little better than these.

There is an increase which is not "the increase of God." The vulgar worldly estimate of success invades the Church, and popular preaching, crowds to listen, wealth, social status, fine buildings, large contributions, vigorous organizations and the like, which shopkeepers would count prosperity in their business, are too often complacently pointed to as signs of a healthy Church. But all these can be attained without one tingle of the Divine life passing through the carcase. Such increase, without the deepening and spread of the quick vitality drawn from Jesus Christ, is not healthy growth, but a diseased wen, which must be excised before soundness returns, or a dropsical swelling which must be reduced. The autumn meadows are full of puff-balls which look white and solid, but have nothing inside but an acrid powder. The difference between these and the ripening fruit in the orchard, is the difference between the increase with which too many Christian communities are pleased, and that which is worthy of being called "the increase of God." It is not hard to build quickly and high, if we are content to take our mortar from the slime-pits, and to make bricks a substitute for stones. But, sooner or later, the lightning will fall on the tower, and the speech of its builders be confounded, and their confederation scattered. The true building can only rise when each stone is built on the one Foundation, and all are held together by no outward bond, but by the life that pulsates through all the courses of the temple that rises through the ages for an habitation of God.

IV. Note the personal hold of Jesus Christ which is the condition of all life and growth.

Nourishment, unity, growth, all come from Him, and are realized by us if we fulfil the plain condition stated in the context, and are "holding the Head." In the vine the sap rises naturally without effort on the part of tendril or leaf, and the life circulates through the body by the automatic and unconscious action of the organs. But these metaphors fail in describing the requisites for the reception of life from Jesus, and we have to make them out with the other symbol of the bride and bridegroom, in which the union of persons is ennobled, because it requires voluntary choice and conscious cleaving of the one to the other, in an effort which itself is blessedness, and is the condition of tasting the fullest sweetness of the purest joy of earth, which in its purity mirrors the heaven bending above loving hearts.

What, then, is the effort which we should put forth in order to secure the flow of Christ's life through ourselves and our Churches? The apostle uses a vigorous word, the force of which may be felt by reference to other instances of its employment. It is used to describe the action of the women after the Resurrection, when they clasped Christ's feet with the grasp of love that had passed in one astounding leap from the depth of misery to the height of rapture. It is used to describe the tight clasp with which the lame men held Peter and John, afraid that, if he let go, he would fall. So it implies a firm, almost desperate clutch, in which Love and Need, like two hands, clasp Him and will not let Him go. Such tenacious grip implies the adhesive energy of the whole nature—the mind laying hold upon truth, the heart clinging to love, the will submitting to authority. It will not be attained and continued without effort. The fingers slacken unless their grasp is continually renewed, and the appeals of sense and of the necessary tasks concerned with the material present, through they may be so answered and done as to bring us nearer to our Lord, may also part us from Him. They will certainly separate us from Him unless we have sacred times in our lives when we shut out the world and renew our hold of Him. The will has much to do with the firmness of a Christian's hold of Christ. If we honestly and earnestly resolve that, God helping us, we will not let the world and the flesh loosen our grasp of Him, we shall have a new criterion for the world's good and evil, a new test for its treasures, a new insight into what is our true felicity. That firm grasp is the indispensable condition of drawing life from Him, and the measure of our adherence to Jesus Christ is the measure of our vitality.

So all the manifold duties of the Christian life come at last to be summed up in this one, of keeping close to Jesus. When Barnabas was sent down to see into the strange new phenomenon of Gentiles who had received Christ, what did he exhort these new converts, just rescued from heathenism, and weak and ignorant, to do? He did not bid them seek to acquire fuller theological knowledge, or to secure an orderly ministry of ordained men, or to organize themselves in proper fashion. All these things, if necessary, would come, if what he did enjoin were done. "He exhorted them all that with purpose of heart they should cleave unto the Lord." Do that, and all else will follow. Hold fast by Him, like the limpet to the rock. He Himself has summed all our duty and pointed the path of safety in His parting invitation, which offers all blessedness, and enjoins a duty which love will find a sweet necessity and purest joy: "Abide in Me, and I in you. As the branch cannot bear fruit of itself, except it abide in the vine; no more can ye, except ye abide in Me."

WISE HASTE.

WISE HASTE.

"See that ye hasten the matter."—2 CHRON. xxiv. 5.

THE young King Joash, under the tutelage of the high priest Jehoiada, made up his mind to attempt a Jewish reformation. The first step was building, or at all events repairing, the neglected and ruinous temple. The king summoned the proper ecclesiastical authorities, by whose default it had come into such a condition, and instructed them immediately to take steps to gather in the necessary contributions. He does not seem to have been quite sure of his men—or, rather, he was tolerably sure of them; for he thought it necessary to stir them with this somewhat curt and stringent exhortation: "See that you do not let the grass grow under your feet; but hasten the matter," namely, the raising of funds. And we are told, notwithstanding, "the Levites hastened it not." Church authorities do not often much like laymen's interference with their prerogatives, and are accustomed to take matters a great deal more easily than the more impetuous outsiders, who are enthusiastic, and seek to quicken official and professional indifference. However, we need not say anything more about Joash and his lazy Levites, but take these words as a very imperative and earnest exhortation to ourselves. "See that ye hasten the matter," whatever it be that God has entrusted to you.

I. There are two kinds of haste, the right and the wrong.

Haste which comes from imperfectly appropriated convictions is wrong. The seed that sprung up quickly did so because it had no depth of earth, and since it had not, it could have no length of root, and because it had no length of root it had nothing to sustain it in the scorching heat and the sunshine, and it withered away. There are many earnest people who are in such a hurry to begin Christian work—in these days of exhortation to good people to be doing something for God—and who make it their occupation so completely, that they have no time to look after the roots of their Christian life, and consequently they bear no fruit worth harvesting. The haste which seeks to abbreviate the preparatory processes of meditation and communion with God, and appropriation of His grace, is unblest haste. And, in regard to its apparent results in matters of Christian effort, the cynical saying in the Book of Proverbs will come true, " An inheritance may be gotten hastily at the beginning ; but the end thereof shall not be blessed."

There is another kind of haste, which is a counterfeit of the true. Hurry pretends to be haste, but it is "half-sister to delay." The quickness which vamps up superficial work is not the conduct enjoined on us in the words of our text. Time spent in digging deep foundations is not lost, though there is nothing above ground to show for it after many days' work. It looks rapid work to run up walls a brick and a half thick, and with scarcely any depth of foundation, but they will fall even more quickly than they were built if a gale blow.

Another kind of spurious haste we are sometimes tempted to fall into, namely, the haste which is sure to tire the worker because he began too fast. In a long foot-race the competitor who is "leading" at the first "lap" is very seldom the winner. It is better to begin at such a pace as we can keep up, than at such as takes away all our breath before we have covered half the course. Look at the workmen who have for ten hours a day to use trowel or hammer. We think that we could do it twice as fast, and quite as thoroughly. So perhaps we could for a few minutes, but when the task has to be kept up all day long, and six days a week, the amateur will find out how much homely wisdom there is in the old proverb, "The more haste the less speed." Something that is "slow to begin, and never ending," is the kind of haste to be recommended. It is easy to light a fire with straw and brown paper, and it will burn up cheerily and brightly long before coals begin to smoke; but which fire will last the longer? "See that ye hasten the matter" by all means; but see, too, that you do not cut short the private, meditative, contemplative side of your Christian life; and see that you do not put in superficial work; and see that you calculate your strength and your persistence wisely, and begin at the same rate as that at which you mean to end. For when the apostle said, "Ye did run well; what did hinder you?" it would have been a true answer if some of the Galatians had replied, "We ran so well at first that that hindered us from keeping up the pace."

II. Consider some of the fields in which the enjoined hastening of the matter is to be put in practice.

If I were now preaching to a congregation that was not so largely composed of professedly Christian people, of course the first thing that I should say would be, "See that you hasten the matter of your own personal acceptance of Jesus Christ as your Saviour." For that is the foundation of all, and "now is the accepted time." There may be some one to whom these words may come, some young man or woman, or perhaps some older person, who has been thinking and hesitating, and all but actually leaning his or her whole trust upon Christ, and who yet has delayed it. "See that *ye* hasten the matter."

But, then, seeing that the most of you are, at all events, nominal Christians, our exhortation is mainly to be directed to the subsequent steps of the Christian life.

For instance, see that nothing comes between us and the immediate abandonment of anything and everything that we know or suspect to be wrong. There are things which cannot be done quickly, and there are some other things which can scarcely be done except quickly, and I doubt whether any man ever plucked up strongly rooted sin or fault unless he did it suddenly, and out and out, and by one supreme effort of will, which loosened the fangs of the roots. You cannot draw decayed teeth gradually. There must be a wrench. Of another of the Jewish religious reformations it is said, "The thing was done suddenly," and therefore it was thoroughly done, and so "all the people rejoiced." When the serpent came out of the heat, "and fastened upon Paul's hand," suppose he had said to himself, "Now, this thing must be done gradually. We must get rid of this evil by degrees; it will not do to hurry the process too much." You cannot take a serpent off a man's arm at the rate of a coil a day, but must shake it into the fire as quickly as possible, with one vigorous motion at once. The beginning of all true conquest of our evil is an instantaneous resolve to cast it from us, followed by immediate, persistent, and unresting action. I know it will be a lifelong work. The embankments meant to bring the erratic course of the river into bounds and to keep in the floods may be swept away and have to be rebuilt. They will certainly want constant watching and frequent strengthening. But the longer and more difficult the work, the more reason for the ringing summons, "See that ye hasten the matter;" since, if a thing is wrong, it cannot be given up too soon, and delay only gives the evil more power.

In like manner, whenever we know a thing to be duty, do not let us delay a second in the performance of it. One of the old psalms says, "I made haste, and delayed not, but made haste to keep Thy commandments." That is the language of all true obedience. When I was a boy, in the days when parental discipline was rather more of a reality than it is now, my father used to say, "My boy, not obedience only, but prompt obedience." Most of us, no doubt, have found out by this time that when a disagreeable duty has to be performed it is best to get it over at once. The more nauseous the draught, the more need there is to gulp it down quickly. No unwelcome tasks become any the less unwelcome by putting them off till to-morrow. It is only when they are behind us and done, that we begin to find that there is a sweetness to be tasted afterwards, and that the remembrance of unwelcome duties unhesitatingly done is welcome and pleasant. Accomplished, they are full of blessing, and there is a smile on their faces as they leave us. Undone, they stand threatening and disturbing our tranquillity, and hindering our communion with God. If there be lying before you, my brother, any bit of work from which you shrink, go straight up to it and do it at once. The only way to get rid of it is to do it. In the quaint dialect of the early Quakers, "to be clear of my burden" meant—to fulfil some hard task which God was felt to have enjoined; and there is no other escape from the pressure of disagreeable duties than this, "See that ye hasten the matter."

I might apply this exhortation of our text in another direction, upon which, however, I do not need to dwell. The original application of the saying was to one form of what has too much monopolized the title of "work for God," namely, efforts directed specially to the diffusion of religion. If men dawdled at their business in the way in which they dawdle at doing their Christian work, they would all be in the bankruptcy court before the year was out. And unless we form a vigorous determination that we shall be like our Master, "unhasting" in the false sense of the word, "but unresting," and promptly filling every moment—and how elastic the moments are!—with the service which the moment requires, we shall pass out of life with very little done. "See that ye hasten the matter."

III. Let me for a moment, before I close, suggest one or two of the plain reasons why such haste as I have been trying to describe is absolutely necessary for us.

There is so much to do, so much in perfecting our own Christian character and in winning the world for our King. "There remaineth yet very much land to be possessed." How little we have accomplished in all these years! How little liker our Master we are than we were five, ten, twenty years ago! How little victory we have won over our besetting weaknesses! How few of the habits that we long ago knew to be deleterious we have got rid of! So much waits and craves to be done. If we are slothful, the devil and his angels are not. Why does the fire-engine go through crowded streets at such a pace? Because the fire is burning at such a pace. Therefore they have to whip the horses into a gallop, and everything has to get out of the way. "See that ye hasten the matter," for the other side hastens its matters with a vengeance—so much remains to be done, and the evil is growing so fast; every moment's delay adds so enormously to its power, and the issues at stake are so tremendous, and the Christian life which is slothful and does the work of the Lord negligently is so vapid, uninteresting, and wearisome to the liver, as compared with one crowded to the very margin with work, and that has no time for unwholesome brooding and melancholy retrospection, because it feels that so much is crying out to be done.

I need not remind you of the example of Jesus Christ and His toilsome life. At the beginning of that Gospel which is practically the Gospel of the Servant, the words seem to hurry one after another, telling the swift succession of toils and services in which He engaged, and how, like beneficent flame, He leaped from one cold, dark misery to another, bringing to each swift radiance and unwonted fire of joy. Observe those "immediatelys" and "forthwiths" and "straightways" that crowd the first pages of Mark's Gospel. And let us take the lesson taught us by Him who Himself recognized that, even in His great work, there was need for diligence, and who Himself has told us that He shared with us one of the motives for hastening the matter which we might have thought could not belong to Him, when He said, "I must work the works of Him that sent Me while it is called day: the night cometh, when no man can work." The night for Thee, blessed Lord! Is there any time for Thee, O Thou Omnipotent Christ, when

Thou canst not work? Yes, a time when, the conditions and limitations and associations of earth having ceased, it was no longer possible for Him to manifest the human sympathy which He delighted to give, nor to alleviate by the touch of His hand the ills that He was willing to bear. Even that thought, that so little time is left us to do so great a work, Jesus Christ shared with us, and we ought to seek to share it with Him.

There is an old curse in the Book against "the men that did the work of the Lord negligently," under the lash of which a great many Christian people to-day will come. And there is an old description in one of the prophets of "the doers of evil," which may well be held up as a rebuke and an exhortation to us in our poor attempts at doing good. We are told that they did it "with both hands earnestly." Some of us are contented to do good with one hand slackly, and some of us will not touch the burden "with the tip of one of our fingers." Shame, that in a universe in which unresting motion is the law of its being, and over which reigns a Father who worketh hitherto, and a Lord who works with His servants, and in which the powers of evil are ever active, the laggards should be those who profess to have been bought with an inestimable price, and to be bound by the strongest and tenderest motives to a service which they discharge so ill! Be not slothful, but work while it is called day, and "see that ye hasten the matter."

PHASES OF FAITH.

PHASES OF FAITH.

"Many believed on Him. Then said Jesus to those Jews which believed on Him . . ."—JOHN viii. 30, 31.

THE Revised Version accurately represents the original by varying the expression in these two clauses, retaining "believed on Him" in the former, and substituting the simple "believed Him" in the latter. The variation in two contiguous clauses can scarcely be accidental in so careful a writer as the Apostle John. And the reason and meaning of it are obvious enough on the face of the narrative. His purpose is to distinguish between more and less perfect acceptance of Jesus Christ. The more perfect is the former, "they believed on Him;" the less perfect is the latter, the simple acceptance of His word on His claim of Messiahship, which is stigmatized as shallow, and proved to be transient by the context.

They were "Jews" which believed, and they continued to be so whilst they were believing. Now, the word "Jew" in this Gospel always connotes antagonism to Jesus Christ; and as for these persons, how slight and unreliable their adhesion to the Lord is, comes out in the course of the next few verses; and by the end of the chapter they are taking up stones to stone Him.

So John would show us that there is a kind of acceptance which may be real, and may be the basis of something much better hereafter, but which, if it does not grow, rots and disappears; and he would draw a broad line of distinction between that and the other mental act, far deeper, more wholesome, more lasting, and vital, which he designates as "believing *on* Him." I take these words, then, for consideration, not so much to make them the basis of my observations, as because they afford me a starting-point for the consideration of the various phases of the act of believing; its blessings and its nature, and its relation to its objects, which are expressed in the New Testament by the various connections and constructions of this word.

Now, the facts with which I wish to deal may be very briefly stated. There are three ways in which the New Testament represents the act of believing, and its relation to its Object, Christ. These three are, first, the simple one which appears in the text as "believed Him." Then there is a second, which appears in two forms, slightly different, but which, for our purpose, may be treated as substantially the same—"believing on Him." And then there is a third, which, literally and accurately translated, is, "believing unto" or "into Him." That phrase is John's favourite one, and rather unfortunately, though perhaps necessarily, it has been generally rendered by our translators by the less forcible "believing in," which gives the idea of repose, but does not give the idea of motion towards. These three, then, I think, do set forth, if we will ponder them, very large lessons as to the essence of this act of believing, as to the Object upon which it fastens, and as to the blessings which flow from it, which it will be worth our while to consider now. I may cast the whole into the shape of three exhortations—believe Him, believe on Him, believe unto Him.

I. First, then, believe Christ.

We accept a man's words when we trust the man. Even if belief, or faith, is represented in the New Testament, as it very rarely is, as having for its object the words of revelation, behind that acceptance of the words lies confidence in the person speaking. And the beginning of all true Christian faith has in it, not merely the intellectual acceptance of certain propositions as true, but a confidence in the veracity of Him by whom they are made known to us—even Jesus Christ our Lord.

I do not need to insist upon that at any length here —it would take me away from my present purpose; but what I do wish to emphasize is, that from the very starting-point, the smallest germ of the most rudimentary and imperfect faith which knits a soul to Jesus Christ has Him for its Object, and is thus distinguished from the mere acceptance of truths which, on other grounds than the authority of the speaker, may legitimately commend themselves to a man.

Then believe Him. Now, that breaks up into two thoughts, which are all that I intend to deduce from it now, although many more might be suggested. The one is this, that the least and the lowest that Jesus Christ asks from us is the entire and unhesitating acceptance of His utterances as final, conclusive, and absolutely true. Whatever more Jesus Christ may be, He is, by His life and words, the Communicator of Divine and certain truth. He is a Teacher, though He is a great deal more. And whatever more Christian faith may be—and it is a great deal more— it requires, at least, the frank and full recognition of the authority of every word that comes from His lips. A Christianity without a creed is a dream. Bones without flesh are very dry, no doubt; but what about flesh without bones? An inert, shapeless mass. You will never have a vigorous and true Christian life if it is to be moulded according to the fantastic dream of these latter days, which tells us that we may take Jesus as the Guide of our conduct and need not mind about what He says to us. "Believe Me" is His requirement. The words of His mouth, and the revelations which He has made in the sweetness of His life, and in all the graciousness of His dealings, are the very unveiling to man of absolute and final and certain truth.

But, then, on the other hand, let us remember that, while all this is most clear and distinct in the teaching of Scripture, it carries us but a very short way. We find, in the instance from which we take our starting-point in this sermon, the broad distinction drawn, and practically illustrated in the conduct of the persons concerned, between the simple acceptance of what Christ says, and a true faith that clings to Him for evermore. And the same kind of disparagement of the lower process of merely accepting His word is found more than once in connection with the same phrases. We find, for instance, the two which are connected in our texts used in a previous conversation between our Lord and His antagonists. When He says to them, "This is the work of God, that ye believe on Him whom He hath sent," they reply, dragging down His claim to a lower level, "What sign showest Thou, that we may see, and believe Thee?" He demanded belief *on* Himself; they answer, "We are ready to *believe you*, on condition that we see something that may make the rendering of our belief a logical necessity for us."

Let us lay to heart the rudimentary and incomplete character of a faith which simply accepts the teaching of Jesus Christ, and does no more. The notion that orthodoxy is Christianity, that a man who does not contradict the teaching of the New Testament is thereby a Christian, is a very old and very perilous and very widespread one. There are plenty of us who have no better claim to be called Christians than this, that we never denied anything that Jesus Christ said, though we are not sufficiently interested in it, I was going to say, even to deny it. This rudimentary faith, which contents itself with the acceptance of the truth revealed, hardens into mere formalism, or liquefies into mere careless indifference as to the very truth that it professes to believe. There is nothing more impotent than creeds which lie dormant in our brains, and have no influence upon our lives. I wonder how many readers of this sermon, who fancy themselves good Christians, do with their creed as the Japanese used to do with their emperor—keep him in a palace behind bamboo screens, and never let him do anything, whilst all the reality of power was possessed by another man, who did not profess to be a king at all. Do you think you are Christians because you would sign thirty-nine or three hundred and ninety articles of Christianity, if they were offered to you, while there is not one of them that influences either your thinking or your conduct? Do not let us have these "sluggish kings," with a mayor of the palace to do the real government, but set on the throne of your hearts the principles of your religion, and see to it that all your convictions be translated into practice, and all your practice be informed by your convictions.

This belief in a set of dogmas, on the authority of Jesus

Christ, about which dogmas we do not care a rush, and which make no difference upon our lives, is the faith that James has so many hard things to say about; and he ventures upon a parallel that I should not like to venture on unless I were made bold by his example: "Thou believest, O vain man; thou doest well: the devils also believe, and"—better than you, in that their belief does something for them they—"believe, and *tremble*." But what shall we say about a man who professes himself a disciple, and neither trembles, nor thrills, nor hopes, nor dreads, nor desires, nor does any single thing because of his creed? Believe Jesus, but do not stop there.

II. Believe on Christ.

Now, as I have remarked already, and as many of you know, there is a slightly different, twofold form of this phrase in Scripture. I need not trouble you with the minute distinction between the one and the other. Both forms coincide in the important point on which I wish to touch. That representation of believing *on* Christ carries us away at once from the mere act of acceptance of His word on His authority to the far more manifestly voluntary, moral, and personal act of reliance upon Him. The metaphor is expanded in various ways in Scripture, and instead of offering any thoughts of my own about it, I would simply ask attention to three of the forms in which it is set forth in the Old and in the New Testaments.

The first of them, and the one which we may regard as governing the others, is that in the book of the Prophet Isaiah, "Behold, I lay in Zion a Stone, a sure Foundation;" and, as the Apostle Peter comments, "He that believeth on Him shall not be confounded." There the figure presented is the superposition of the building upon its Foundation, the rest of the soul, and the rearing of the life on the basis of Jesus Christ.

How much that metaphor says to us about Him, as the Foundation, in all the aspects in which we can apply that term! He is the Basis of our hope, the Guarantee of our security, the Foundation-stone of our beliefs, the very Ground on which our whole life reposes, the Source of our tranquillity, the Pledge of our peace. All that I think, feel, desire, wish, and do, ought to be rested upon that dear Lord, and builded there by simple faith. By patient persistence of effort rearing up the fabric of my life firmly upon Him, and grafting every stone of it—if I might so use the metaphor—into the bedding-stone, which is Christ, I shall be strong, peaceful, and pure.

The storm comes, the waters rise, the winds howl, the hail and the rain "sweep away the refuge of lies," and the dwellers in these frail and foundationless houses are hurrying in wild confusion from one peak to another, before the steadily rising tide. But he that builds on that Foundation "shall not make haste," as Isaiah has it; shall not need to hurry to shift his quarters before the flood overtake him; shall look out serene upon all the hurtling fury of the wild storm, and the rise of the sullen waters. So, reliance on Christ, and the honest making of Him the Basis, not of our hopes only, but of our thinkings and of our doings, and of our whole being, is the secret of security, and the pledge of peace.

Then there is another form of the same phrase, "believing on," in which is suggested not so much the figure of building upon a foundation, as of some feeble man resting upon a strong stay, or clinging to an outstretched and mighty arm. The same metaphor is implied in the word "reliance." We lean upon Christ when, forsaking all other props, and realizing His sufficiency and sweetness, we rest the whole weight of our weariness and all the impotence of our weakness upon His strong and unwearied arm, and so are saved. All other stays are like that one to which the prophet compares the King of Egypt—the papyrus reed in the Nile stream, on which, if a man leans, it will break into splinters which will go into his flesh, and make a poisoned wound. But if we lean on Christ, we lean on a brazen wall and an iron pillar, and anything is possible sooner than that that stay shall give.

There is still another form of the metaphor, in which neither building upon a foundation, nor leaning upon a support which is thought of as below what rests upon it, is suggested, but rather the hanging upon something firm and secure which is above what hangs from it. The same picture is suggested by our word "dependence." "As a nail fastened in a sure place," said one of the prophets, "on Him shall hang all the glory of His Father's house."

"Hangs my helpless soul on Thee."

The rope lowered over the cliffs supports the adventurous bird-nester in safety above the murmuring sea. They who clasp Christ's hand outstretched from above, may swing over the deepest, most vacuous abyss, and fear no fall.

So, brother, build on Christ, rely on Him, depend on Him, and it shall not be in vain. But if you will not build on the sure Foundation, do not wonder if the rotten one gives way. If you will not lean on the strong Stay, complain not when the weak one crumbles to dust beneath your weight. And if you choose to swing over the profound depth at the end of a piece of pack-thread, instead of holding on by an adamantine chain wrapped round God's throne, you must be prepared for its breaking and your being smashed to pieces below.

III. The last exhortation that comes out of this comparative study of these phrases is—Believe into Christ.

That is a very pregnant and remarkable expression, and it can scarcely, as you see, be rendered into our language without a certain harshness; but still it is worth while to face the harshness for the sake of getting the double signification that is involved in it. For when we speak of "believing unto or into Him," we suggest two things, both of which, apparently, were in the minds of the writers of the New Testament. One is motion towards, and the other is repose in, that dear Lord.

So, then, true Christian faith is the flight of the soul towards Christ. Therein is one of the special blessednesses of the Christian life, that it has for its object and aim absolutely infinite and unattainable completeness and glory, so that unwearied freshness, inexhaustible buoyancy, endless progress, are the dower of every spirit that truly trusts in Christ. All other aims and objects are limited, transient, and will be left behind. Every other landmark will sink beneath the horizon, where so many of our landmarks have sunk already, and where they will all disappear when the last moment comes. But we may have, and if we are Christian people we shall have, borne before us, sufficiently certain of being reached to make our efforts hopeful and confident, sufficiently certain of never being reached to make our efforts blessed with endless aspirations, the great light and love of that dear Lord, to yearn after whom is better than to possess all besides, and following hard after whom, even in the very motion there is rest, and in the search there is finding. Religion is the flight of the soul, the aspiration of the whole man after the unattainable Attainable—"that I may know Him, and be found in Him."

Oh, how such thoughts ought to shame us who call ourselves Christians! Growth, progress, getting nearer to Christ, yearning ever with a great desire after Him!—do not the words seem irony when applied to most of us? Think of the average type of sluggish contentment with present attainments that marks Christian people; tortoises in their crawling rather than eagles in their flight.

And let us take our portion of shame, and remember that the faith which believes Him, and that which believes on Him, both need to be crowned and perfected by that which believes towards Him; of which the motto is, "Forgetting the things that are behind, I reach forward to the things that are before."

But there is another side to this last phase of faith. That true believing towards or unto Christ is the rest of the soul in Him. By faith that deep and most real union of the believing soul with Jesus Christ is effected which may be fitly described as our entrance into and abode in Him. The believer is as if incorporated into Him in whom he believes. Indeed, the apostle ventures to use a more startling expression than *incorporation* when he says that "he that is joined to the Lord is one Spirit." If by faith we press towards, by faith we shall be in Christ. Faith is at once motion and rest, search and finding, desire and fruition. The felicity of this last form of speech is its expression of both these ideas, which are united in fact as in word. A rare construction of the verb *to believe*, with the simple preposition *in*, coincides with this part of the meaning of *believing unto* or *into*, and need not be separately considered.

With this understanding of its meaning, we see how natural is John's preference for this construction. For surely, if he has anything to tell us, it is that the true Christian life is a life enclosed, as it were, in Jesus Christ. Nor need I remind you how Paul, though he starts from a different point of view, yet coincides with John in this teaching. For, to him, to be " in Christ " is the sum of all blessedness, righteousness, peace, and power. As in an atmosphere, we may dwell in Him. He may be the strong Habitation to which we may continually resort. One of the Old Testament words for trusting means taking refuge, and such a thought is naturally suggested by this New Testament form of expression. "I flee unto Thee to hide me." In that Fortress we dwell secure.

To be in Jesus, wedded to Him by the conjunction of will and desire, wedded to Him in the oneness of a believing spirit and in the obedience of a life, to be thus in Christ is the crown and climax of faith, and the condition of all perfection. To be in Christ is life; to be out of Him is death. In Him we have redemption; in Him we have wisdom, truth, peace, righteousness, hope, confidence. To be in Him is to be in heaven. We enter by faith. Faith is not the acceptance merely of His Word, but is the reliance of the soul on Him, the flight of the soul towards Him, the dwelling of the soul in Him. "Come, My people, into thy chambers, and shut thy doors about thee . . . until the indignation be overpast."

TENT AND ALTAR.

TENT AND ALTAR.

"Abram pitched his tent, . . . and there he builded an altar."—GEN. xii. 8.

ENTERING the land of Canaan from the north, as an emigrant from Harran would do, Abram and his company passed southwards, through the possessions of a civilized and settled race, till they reached the fertile country round Shechem, and there, in a place the luxuriant beauty of which would excite the wanderer's desire to call it his, as much as the tokens on every side of an established order would shake his confidence in his power to win it, the Divine promise was renewed. God chooses the right scenes and times for His appearances, and the very fact that Abram again received the promise of the land at the "terebinth of Moreh" implies that he then specially needed it. The reason for the gracious repetition is told us: "And the Canaanite was then in the land." Abram was brought into contact with the fierce strength which had to be met and crushed before the land could be his, and no doubt he quailed at the prospect. Therefore "the Lord appeared unto Abram, and said, Unto thy seed will I give the land." The reiterated assurance and the distant date assigned for its fulfilment would strengthen his faith and lessen his fears. Therefore with lightened heart, absolved from conflict with the Canaanites by the terms of the promise designating future generations as the conquerors, he reared an altar beside the sacred tree, to "Jehovah who appeared unto him." Quickened faith thankfully commemorates God's tender fostering of tremulous faith.

But Shechem was not to be his goal. In this first journey Abram seems to intend a survey of the whole territory, and therefore he passed on still southwards towards what was afterwards to be called Bethel, and to bear a name sacred and dear in all centuries and countries. On the stony hillside to the east of Bethel, a stern contrast to the smiling fertility of Shechem, he stayed for a time, a temporary encampment there being probably less likely to be disputed than in the better place, and there once more he pitched his tent, and once more built an altar—whether for sacrifice, or like that at his previous station, simply as a memorial and declaration of his faith, does not appear. It is sufficient for our purpose to note the combination of these two acts, by which Abram inaugurated his first halting-place for any lengthened stay, and as it were took possession of the land for himself and for Jehovah. The combination may suggest some useful lessons.

I. All life should blend the earthly and the heavenly. As soon as the tent is pitched, and the necessities of bodily life in some measure satisfied, the next thing is the altar of God.

Religion is meant to run through the whole of common life, not to be crowded and clotted in corners, leaving the rest of our days empty and unblessed by it. It is all very well to pray and praise and preach on Sundays; what about Saturday and Monday? It is all very well to call ourselves Christians, and to profess to belong to some ecclesiastical body or other; what about the daily life? Is my prayer only a matter of fixed times and perhaps formal words, or are all my days devotion? Abram twined these two aspects of life in most intimate union, not only in this instance but habitually; and therein is an example for us, who are so far in advance of him as regards the objects of our religion. He did not know nearly as much about God as we do; he was not as favoured with teaching of the lofty and spiritual side of religion as we are. His faith was very imperfect as far as its contents are concerned, but it had a penetrative and diffusive power in it; perhaps to some extent owing to its less transcendent and lofty character, which may well shame us, who, with a fuller knowledge, and the material for a loftier and more all-pervasive faith, manage to make such ghastly separation between the two halves of the devout life, and keep the heavenly and its principles so widely apart from the earthly and its practices. There is no sanity, nor sweetness, nor nobleness in earthly life, unless through and through, as light is flashed into some dull, dense, watery cloud, it be shot and interpenetrated with the light of the mighty and ennobling principles that flow from the gospel; and no religion is worth being called so, nor has it any pith of reality in it, unless it has force to press into the most close-grained solids and most minute trifles, and into them to infuse its hallowing and ennobling spirit, working like lifting leaven on lumpish dough. By the side of every tent in which we dwell we should raise an altar to God.

To-day, millenniums after this man lived, and amongst people who do not share either his faith or ours, namely, the Mohammedan populations of the East, the name for Abraham is "the Friend"—the Friend of God, that is.

The expression is borrowed from Scripture. Whatever besides that name may express, this at all events is distinctly set forth by it, that the salient characteristics of the patriarch's life was close and habitual intimacy with God. That communion did not interfere with the whole-hearted discharge of common duties, the simple enjoyment of common blessings, or the heroic readiness to rise to difficult heights of uncommon sacrifice or effort. Like all the Old Testament "saints," he came "eating and drinking," marrying and giving in marriage, buying and selling and getting gain, and practising in all a wholesome religion which sought for no solitary, supercilious, or selfish separateness, but

> "Travelled on life's common way
> In cheerful godliness,"

filling all occupations and circumstances with a new spirit, and so finding in things of smallest worth materials for a sacrifice more costly than much fine gold. The fact that he and all these Old Testament "saints" were "men of affairs," and not recluses, and that their religion did not impel them to a new mode of life, but to a new way of doing the old things, may well teach us how close the blending of our religious and our common life should be.

But not only do Abraham and the men of faith, who lived by faith before it had a historical Christ to grasp, read us this lesson. The worshippers of less pure gods do so too. It is not often that one finds a Christian as little ashamed of practising his religion and presenting his worship before unsympathizing onlookers as Turks or idolaters are. True, the very fact that to them religion is so much a matter of external observance makes it easier for them to practise the external observances in any circumstances. But, making all allowance for that, I venture to say that there is not a false faith on the face of the earth which does not preach a lesson and administer a rebuke to us Christian people in regard of this one matter, the way in which religion and life—a very poor religion, no doubt, and a very imperfect life—touch each other at all points; and because they thus touch, are really one.

Does our better religion so interpenetrate our lives? Have we this same experience of making every act worship, and of carrying the motives and strengths drawn from our gospel into every corner of our daily life. Go back in thought over to-day. Can you lay your finger upon a single act that you have done to-day which would have been done differently if you had not believed that Jesus Christ loved you? Can you lay your finger upon any inclination that you have abstained from gratifying because you knew that loyalty to Him forbade your yielding? I hope the answer is not in the negative universally; but oh, how faint, how few, scattered through our lives like points, or as stars thinly sown in the vacant regions of the sky, are the moments and the acts in which we have lived like Christians, and carried our religion into our shops and commerce, and our studies and our daily duties!

Let us take the pattern from Abram, who " pitched his tent, and builded an altar."

II. Another lesson may be suggested. The family should be a Church.

In the old patriarchal times, before priesthood had attained to any development, the head of the family or clan, the patriarch, was priest. Abram built the altar, and Abram offered the sacrifice. In the New Testament we find a number—relatively a large number, and absolutely a considerable number, of households—all the members of which were Christians. We read, too, of more than one instance in the house of some Christian, which expression must at least include the idea of domestic worship and household religion, whether other Christians than those of the family belonged to that "Church" or no. In days not beyond the memories—the thankful memories—of some of us, it was understood that a Christian household was one in which the father and mother taught their children. It was considered, too, that it meant a household in which there was family worship.

Now although I do not know, and therefore will not take upon me to affirm, I do shrewdly suspect and therefore venture to ask, whether these things are so now as generally as they once were. I wonder how many households in our class of Christian society there are, in which father and mother think that they have done their duty to their children when they have sent them to the Sunday school, while they are idle at home; and I wonder how many there are who never open their lips in their houses, as leading the devotions of their family. Suffer the word of exhortation. I believe that one reason why some aspects of religious life are dark and unpromising at this time is the decay of family religion as expressed in family worship and family instruction in the households of professing Christians. "Abram pitched his tent, and builded an altar."

III. Further, let me ask you to note here the illustration of another thought. God should get our best.

A black camel's-hair tent, with a couple of sticks at either end of it to hold up the roof, and a peg or two in the ground to fasten the ropes to, was neither expensive nor difficult to set up. Ten minutes would do that. That was quite enough for Abram. But he gathered the great stones of the place together, and *built* the altar. As for the tent, it is sufficient that it be pitched anywhere, with little expenditure of time and trouble. It is to come down to-morrow, and while it stands its purpose is only the shelter of myself. But as for the altar, with toil and strain of muscle, and many a deep breath and drop of sweat from the brow, roll the great stones together, and lay them true, without trace of tool on them, but majestic in simplicity, to witness to the massive solidity of the faith which reared them, and the unadorned, uncontaminated purity of the revelation of the God for whose worship they were laid.

"Lo! I dwell within cedar, and the ark of the Lord dwells within curtains," said David. Whose fault was that, David? Did you not build the house of cedar before you thought about a house for God? We do the opposite of what Abram did. Most of us build our own houses, and, if there are any stones left over, are good enough to spare them for building some altar to God. We give Him the superfluities. We allow Him the second place, thinking about self first; and so losing all the blessings of thorough consecration and noble surrender, and of yielding up what is highest to Him who is the Highest. Give God the best —that is the minimum of duty; for unless we do, we give Him nothing.

> "Give all thou canst!
> High Heaven rejects the lore
> Of nicely calculated less or more."

Do not think that anything of your own is worthy of as sedulous care, as generous bestowment, as intense effort, as thorough devotion, as is the service of the Lord. I do not mean in material things only, because the true wealth of a man is not the abundance of the things that he possesses, and that best which we are to give to God is not merely the best portion of the things that belong to us, but the best devotion of our hearts—their best affections; the strongest resolve of obedient wills, the intensest desire of aspiring spirits, the fullest consecration of surrendered lives, the firmest confidence of reliant, and therefore loving and obedient hearts. Give God the superiorities of your nature, whatever you keep for yourselves; and try so to blend the motive of devotion to Him with all action of heart and mind, as that there shall be nothing retained from Him to whom the best is consciously given.

IV. Lastly, this incident may suggest to us how building for God lasts, while building for ourselves perishes.

The tent has disappeared; the altar remains. I dare say these stones half-way between Bethel and Ai are there still, standing where and as Abram piled them, though hard to find, and impossible to identify amid the rocks and ruins that strew the face of the land around. What has become of his tent? It was pitched for a little while. In his nomad life it was struck soon, and no trace remained but a little heap of rubbish, and a circle of charred ashes where the fire had glinted cheerily for a day or two. All was gone but the altar. In the great cities of antiquity which the spade is now laying bare for us, what has become of the houses which the people built for themselves? Gone—where the snow and the rain of the years when they were built have gone. It is the temples that are left, in the marsh which is now where Ephesus once was; in the desolation which is now where Babylon once was; beneath the mounds which are now where Heliopolis once was. The houses of the people are gone; the temples of the gods remain. Which things are an allegory. "He that soweth to the flesh shall of the flesh reap," and of selfish lives there will be nothing left but a foul flavour and a bad memory. "The world passeth away, and the fashion thereof: he that doeth the will of God shall abide for ever." It was Abraham's religion that made him dwell in tents. He came from a settled civilization, where there were cities, as we can see in the narratives. He came into a settled civilization, where there was city life, and plenty of stone houses if he had chosen to go into them. "He dwelt in tabernacles; for he looked for the city which hath the foundations, whose Builder and Maker is God." If we in like manner have come to fix and anchor our lives on the only permanent, and to feel ourselves parts of that great order which lives beyond the grave and above the stars, we shall be penetrated with a sense of the transiency of all things here below, and so be well contented to pitch but a moving tent for ourselves, if we can, by God's grace, lay were it even one stone in the temple which, through all the ages, is rising, on the one Foundation, unto Him.

FORGIVING SON OF MAN.

THE FORGIVING SON OF MAN.

"That ye may know that the Son of man hath power on earth to forgive sins, (then saith He to the sick of the palsy,) Arise, take up thy bed, and go unto thine house."—MATT. ix. 6.

THE great example of our Lord's teaching, which we call the Sermon on the Mount, is followed in this and the preceding chapter by a similar collection of His works. These are arranged by the evangelist with some care in three groups, each consisting of three miracles, and separated from each other by other matter. The miracle to which our text refers is the last member of the second triad, of which the others are the stilling of the tempest and the casting out of demons from the two men in the country of the Gadarenes.

One can discern a certain likeness in these three incidents. In all of them our Lord appears as the Peace-bringer. But the spheres in which He works are different in each. The calm which was breathed over the stormy lake was peace, but of a lower kind than that which filled the souls of the demoniacs when the power that agitated them and made discord within had been cast out. Even that peace was lower in kind than that which brought repose by assurance of pardon to this poor paralytic. Forgiveness is a loftier blessing than even the casting out of demons. The manifestation of power and love rises steadily to a climax.

The text subordinates the mere miracle to the authoritative assurance of pardon, and thus teaches us that the most important part of the incident is not the healing of disease, but the accompanying forgiveness of sins. Here we have noteworthy instruction given by our Lord Himself as to the relation between His miracles and that perpetual work of His, which He is doing through the ages and to-day, and will do for us, if we will let Him. It towers high above the miracle, and the miracle is honoured by being its attestation. We deal, then, with this narrative as suggesting great principles over and above the miraculous fact.

I. Man's deepest need is forgiveness.

How strangely irrelevant and wide of the mark seems Christ's response to the eager zeal of the bearers and the pleading silence of the sufferer! "Son,"—or as the original might more accurately and tenderly be rendered, "Child,"—"be of good cheer; thy sins be forgiven thee." That sounded far away from their want. It was far away from their wish; but it was the direct answer to the man's true need. Possibly in this case the disease was the result of early profligacy—

"A sin of flesh avenged in kind."

Probably, too, the paralytic felt, whatever his four kindly neighbours may have done, that what he needed most was pardon; for Christ casts not His pearls before eyes that cannot see their lustre, nor offers His gift of pardon to hearts unwounded by the consciousness of sin. The long hours of compelled inactivity may have been not unvisited by remorseful memories, and the conscience may have stirred in proportion as the limbs stiffened. Be that as it may, it is to be observed that our Lord points to the miracle as a proof of His power to pardon, given not to the palsied man, but to the cavillers standing by, as if the former needed no proof, but had grasped the assurance while it was yet unverified. Thus both Christ's declaration and the swift acceptance of it seem to imply that in that motionless form stretched on its pallet an inward tempest of penitence and longing raged, which could only be stilled by something far deeper than any bodily healing.

At all events, the plain lesson from Christ's treatment of the case is that our deepest need is pardon. Is not our relation to God the most important and deep-reaching relation that we sustain? If that be right, will not everything else come right? As long as that is wrong, will not everything be wrong? And is it not true that, whatever may be our surface diversities, we all have this in common, that we are sinners? King and clown, philosopher and fool, cultured and ignorant, are alike in this, that "all have sinned, and come short of the glory of God." Royal robes and fustian jackets cover the same human heart, which in all is gone astray, and in all writhes more or less consciously under the same unrest, the consequence and token of separation from God.

Hence is seen the wisdom of Christ and the adaptation of His gospel to all men, in that it does not trifle with symptoms, but goes direct to the deep-lying and often latent disease. It is waste time and energy to dally with surface and consequential evils. The only way of making the fruit good is to make the tree good, and then it will bring forth according to its kind. Cooling draughts and water-beds are alleviations for the sick, but the cure must be something more potent. The fontal source of sorrow is sin, for even to the most superficial observation, the greater part of every man's misery comes either from his own wrong-doing or from that of others; and, for the rest of it, the judgment of faith which accepts the declaration of God regards it as needed because of sin, in order to discipline and purify.

The first thing to do in order to stanch men's wounds and redress their misery is to make them pure, and the first thing to do in order to make them pure is to assure them of God's forgiveness for their past impurity. So the sarcasms which are often launched at religious men for "taking tracts to people when they want bread," and the like, are excessively shallow, and simply indicate that the critic has but superficially diagnosed the disease, and is therefore woefully wrong about the needed medicine. God forbid that we should say a word that even seemed to depreciate the value of other forms of philanthropic effort, or to be lacking in sympathy and admiration for the enthusiasm that fills and guides many self-sacrificing and earnest workers amid the squalor and vice of our complex and half-barbarous "civilization." It is the plain duty of Christian people heartily to rejoice in and to help all such work, and to recognize it as good and blessed, being as it is a direct consequence of the Christian view of the solidarity of humanity and of the stewardship of possession. But we must go a great deal deeper than æsthetic, or intellectual, or political, or economic reforms can reach before we touch the real reason why men are miserable. The black well-head must be stanched, or it is useless trying to drain the bog and make its quaking morass solid, fertile soil. We shall effectually and certainly cure the misery only when we begin where the misery begins, and where

Christ began, and deal first with sin. The true "saviour of society" is he who can go to his paralyzed and wretched brother, and, as a minister declaring God's heart, can say to him, "Be of good cheer; thy sins be forgiven thee." Then the palsy will go out of the shrunken limbs, and a new energy will come into them, and the sufferer will rise, take up his bed, and walk.

II. Forgiveness is exclusively a Divine act.

We read that there were sitting by, with jealous and therefore blind eyes, a company of learned men, religious formalists of the first water, gathered, as one of the other evangelists tells us, out of every corner of the land, as a kind of ecclesiastical inquisition, or board of triers, to report on this young Galilæan Teacher, whom His disciples unauthorizedly called Rabbi. They were unmoved by the dewy pity in Christ's gaze as by the nascent hope beginning to swim up into the paralytic's dim eyes. But they had a keen scent for heresy, and so they fastened with sure instinct on the one questionable point, "This man speaketh blasphemies. Who can forgive sins but God only?" Formalists, whose religion is mainly a bundle of red tape tied round men's limbs to keep them from getting at things that they would like, are blind as bats to the radiant beauty of lofty goodness, and insensible as rocks to the wants of sad humanity.

But still these scribes and doctors were perfectly right in the principle which they conceived Jesus to be outraging. Forgiveness is an exclusively Divine act. Of course it is so. Sin is the perversion of our relation to God. The word "sin" implies God, and is meaningless unless the deed be thought of in reference to Him. The same act may be regarded as being sin, or crime, or vice. As sin, it has to do with God; as crime, it has to do with public law and with other men; as vice, it has to do with the standard of morality, and may affect myself alone. The representatives of national law can pardon crime. The impersonal tribunal of morals is silent as to the forgiveness of vice. God alone has to do with vice or crime considered as sin, and He alone against whom only we have sinned can pardon our transgression.

God only can forgive sins, because the essential in forgiveness is not the remission of external penalty, but the unrestrained flow of love from the offended heart of Him who has been sinned against. When you fathers and mothers forgive your children, does the pardon consist simply in sparing the rod? Does it not much rather consist in this, that your love is neither deflected nor embittered any more, by reason of your child's wrong-doing, but pours on the little rebel, as before the fault? So God's forgiveness is at bottom, "Child, there is nothing in My heart to thee but pure and perfect love." Our sins fill the sky with mists, through which the sun itself cannot but look a red ball of lurid fire. But it shines on the upper side of the mists all the same and all the time, and thins them away and scatters them utterly, and shines forth in its own brightness on the rejoicing heart. Pardon is God's love, unchecked and unembittered, granted to the wrong-doer. That is a Divine act exclusively. The carping doctors were quite right; "no man can forgive sins but God only."

Such forgiveness may coexist with the retention of some penalties for the forgiven sin. "Thou wast a God that forgavest them, and Thou tookest vengeance on their inventions." When sins are crimes they are generally punished: The penalties of sins considered as vices or breaches of the standard of morality are always left. For the evil thing done has entered into the complex whole of the doer's past, and its "natural issues" are not averted, though their character is modified, when they are borne in consciousness of God's forgiveness. Then they become merciful chastisement, and therefore tokens of the Father's love. The true penalty of evil, considered as sin, is wholly abolished for the man whom God forgives, for that penalty is separation from God, which is the only real death, and he who is pardoned and knows that he is, knows also that he is joined to God by the pouring on him, unworthy, of that infinitely placable and patient love. Pardon is love rising above the black dam which we have piled up between us and God, and flooding our hearts with its glad waters.

We might add here, though it be somewhat apart from our direct purpose, that the forgiveness of sin is a possibility, in spite of modern declarations that it is not. Many confident voices say so now, and when we venture to ask, with the humility which becomes a mere believer in Christianity when addressing our modern wise men, why forgiveness is impossible, we are referred to the iron links of necessary connection between a man's present and his past, and assured that in such a universe as we live in, neither God nor man can prevent the seed sown from springing, and the sower from reaping what he has sown. But we may take heart to answer that we, too, believe that "whatsoever a man soweth that shall he also reap," and then may ask what that has to do with the Scripture doctrine of forgiveness, which leaves that solemn law quite untampered with, in so far as the iron links which the objectors contemplate are concerned, and proclaims this as the very heart of God's pardon, that the sinful man, who forsakes his sin and trusts in Christ's sacrifice, will be treated as if his sin were non-existent, in so far as it could interfere with the flow of the full tide of God's love.

But we need a definite conveyance of this Divine forgiveness to ourselves. If we have ever been down into the cellars of our own hearts and seen the ugly things that creep and sting there, a vague trust in a vague mercy from a half-hidden God will not be enough for us. The mere peradventure that God is merciful is too shadowy to grasp, and too flimsy for a troubled conscience to lean on. Nothing short of the King's own pardon, sealed with His own seal, is valid; and unless we can come into actual contact with God, and hear, somehow, with infallible certitude from His own lips His assurance of forgiveness, we shall not have enough for our souls' needs.

III. Christ claims and exercises this Divine prerogative of forgiveness.

The fact that Jesus answered the muttered thought of these critics might have convinced them that He exercised other Divine prerogatives, and read men's hearts with a clearer eye than ours. *He* must be rightly addressed as "Lord" of whom it can be said, "There is not a word in my tongue, but, lo, Thou knowest it altogether." If He possess the Divine faculty of reading hearts, He is entitled to exercise the Divine power of forgiving what He discerns there.

But mark His answer to the objectors. He admits their premises completely. They said, "No man can forgive sins, but God only." Now, if Jesus were only a man like the rest of us, standing in the same relation to God as other saints, prophets, and teachers, and having nothing more to do with God's forgiveness than simply to say to a troubled heart, as any of us might do, "Brother, cheer up; I tell you that God forgives you and all who seek His pardon;" if His words to the paralytic were, in His intention, only ministerial and declaratory;—then He was bound, by all the obligations of a religious Teacher, to turn to the objectors and tell them that they misapprehended His meaning. Why did He not say to them in effect, "I speak blasphemies! No, I do not mean that. I know that God alone forgives, and I am only telling our poor brother here, as you might also do, that He does. The blasphemy exists only in your misunderstanding of My meaning"? But Christ's answer is not in the least like this, though every sane and devout teacher of religion would certainly have answered so. In effect He says, "You are quite right. No man can forgive sins, but God only. I forgive sins. Then whom think ye that I, the Son of man, am? I claim to forgive sins. It is easy to make such a claim, easier than to claim power to raise this sick man from his bed, because you can see whether his rising follows the word, whereas the other claim cannot be visibly substantiated. Both sentences are equally easy to say, both things equally impossible for a man to do; only the doing of the one is visible, and of the other is not. I will do the visible impossibility, and then you can judge whether I have the right which I allege to do the invisible one."

Clearly there is in this answer of Jesus a distinct claim to forgive sins as God does. The objection which He meets and the manner of meeting it alike forbid us to take "power to forgive sins" in this context in any but the highest Divine sense. Now, this claim seems to bring us face to face with a very distinct alternative, which I venture to urge on your consideration. To offer the choice of being impaled on one or other horn of a dilemma is not the best way of convincing hesitating minds of the truth; but still it is fair, and to some may be cogent, to say that a very weighty "either . . . or" is here forced on us. Either the Pharisees were right, and Jesus Christ, the meek, the humble, the religious Sage, the Pattern of all self-abnegation, the sweet reasonableness of whose teaching eighteen centuries have not exhausted nor obeyed, was an audacious blasphemer, or He was God manifest in the flesh. The whole incident compels us, in all honest interpretation, to take His words to the sick man as the Pharisees took them, as being the claim to exercise an exclusively Divine prerogative. He assumed power to blot out a man's transgressions, and vindicated the assumption, not on the ground that He was but declaring or bringing the Divine forgiveness, but on the ground that He could do what no mere man could. If Jesus Christ said and did anything like what this narrative ascribes to Him— and if we know anything at all about Him, we know that He did so—there is no hypothesis as to Him which can save His character for the reverence of mankind, but that which sees in Him the Word made flesh, the world's Judge, from whom the world may receive, and from whom alone it can certainly receive, Divine forgiveness.

IV. Jesus Christ brings visible witnesses of His invisible power to forgive sins.

Of course the miracle of healing the paralytic was such evidence in very complete and special form, inasmuch as it and the forgiveness which it was wrought to attest were equally Divine acts, beyond the reach of man's power. We may note, too, that our Lord here teaches us the relative importance of these two, subordinating the miraculous healing to the higher work of giving pardon. But we may permissibly extend the principle, and point to the subsidiary external effects of Christianity in the material and visible sphere of things as attestations of its inward power, which only he who feels his burden of sin falling from his shoulders at the cross knows as a matter of experience. The manifest effects of the Christian faith on individuals, and of the less complete Christian faith which is diffused through society, do stand as strong proofs of the reality of Christ's claim to exercise the power to forgive. The visible results of every earnest effort to carry the gospel to men, and the effects produced in the lives of the recipients, do create an immense presumption in favour of the reality of the power which the gospel proclaims that Jesus exercises. We may admit the extravagance, the coarseness, the narrowness, which too often deform such efforts, and dwarf the spiritual stature of their converts; but when the bitterest criticism has blown away much as froth, is there not left in the cup a great deal which looks and tastes very like the new wine of the kingdom? Passions tamed, hopes hallowed, new and noble direction given to aspirations, self subdued, the charities of life springing like flowers where were briers and thorns or waste barrenness, homes made Bethels, houses of God, that were pandemoniums,—these and the like are the witnesses that Jesus Christ advanced no rash claims, nor raised hopes which He could not fulfil, when He said, "Thy sins be forgiven thee." Wherever Christ's forgiving power enters a heart, life is beautified, purified, and ennobled, and secondary material benefits follows in its train. We have a right to claim the difference between so-called Christian and non-Christian lands as attestations of the reality of Christ's saving work. It is a valid answer to much of the doubt of to-day;—If you wish to see His credentials, look around. His own answer to John's messengers still remains applicable: "Go and tell John the things that ye see and hear." There are miracles, palpable and visible, still wrought by Jesus Christ, more convincing than were those to which the forerunner was directed when his faith faltered. It is still true that "His name, through faith in His name, makes men whole," and that in presence of unbelievers, who may test the cure. Still the dead are raised, deaf ears are opened, dormant faculties are quickened, and, in a thousand channels, the quick spirit of life flows from Jesus, and "everything lives whithersoever that river cometh." Let any system of belief or of no-belief do the like if it can. This rod has budded, at all events. Let the modern successors of Jannes and Jambres, who have found out that Christianity is a "creed outworn," and Jesus an exhausted Source of power, do the same with their enchantments.

These thoughts yield two very plain lessons. One is addressed to professing followers of Jesus Christ. You say that you have received in the depths of your spirit the touch of His forgiving hand, blotting out your sins. Nobody can tell whether you have or not but by observing your life. Does it look as if your profession were true? The world takes its notions of Christianity a great deal more from you, its professors, than it does from preachers or apologists. You are the books of evidences which most men read. See to it that your lives worthily represent the redeeming power of your Lord, and that men, looking at your beautiful, holy, and gentle life, may be constrained to say, "There must be something in the religion that makes him such a man."

The other lesson is for us all. Since we are all alike in that forgiveness is our deepest need, let us seek to have that prime and fundamental necessity supplied first of all; and since Jesus Christ assures us that He exercises the Divine prerogative of forgiveness, and gives us materials for verifying His claim by the visible results of His power, let us all go to Him for the pardon which we need most of all our needs, and which He and only He can give us. Do not waste your time in trying to purify the stream of your lives, miles down from its source; but let Him heal it, and make the bitter waters sweet at the Fountain-head. Do not fancy, friend, that your palsy or your fever, your paralysis of will towards good, or the diseased ardour with which you follow evil and the consequent restless misery, can be healed anywhere besides. Go to Christ, the forgiving Christ, and let Him lay His hand upon you, and from His own sweet and infallible lips listen to the blessed words that shall work like a charm in all your nature, "Son, be of good cheer; thy sins be forgiven thee;" "Daughter, thy faith hath made thee whole; depart in peace." Then shall the eyes of the blind be opened, then shall the lame man leap as an hart, and the tongue of the dumb sing. Then limitations, sorrows, and the diseases of the spirit shall pass away, and forgiveness will bear fruit in joy and power, in holiness, health, and peace.

CHRIST'S "VERILY, VERILY."

CHRIST'S "VERILY, VERILY."

"Verily, verily, I say unto you."—JOHN i. 51.

WE owe the preservation of this remarkable form of asseveration to this evangelist. In the other Gospels the single "Verily" habitually appears, but the double never; while in John's Gospel the double occurs some twenty-five times, and the single not at all. Most of us are, no doubt, aware that the word rendered "Verily" is the simple "Amen," which properly means "firm" or "steadfast." It is used sometimes to confirm an assertion which follows it, and sometimes to sum up a prayer which precedes it. In the former case its force is, "Thus it certainly is;" in the latter it may be paraphrased, "So may it be." Its reduplication gives emphasis, and may be regarded as a superlative, "Most certainly." This doubled form of the phrase is used by Christ only. It becomes no other lips. It may be useful to ponder its significance, and to bring together the various declarations which our Lord heralds by this solemn attestation. We may learn from the study lessons of three kinds — as to the authority of the Teacher, the certainty and importance of His teaching, and as to the duty of the scholars.

I. First, then, we note what that doubled "Verily" claims for the Teacher.

Nothing is more remarkable and distinctive in our

Lord's words than their air of authority, combined with the most perfect gentleness, meekness, and humility. He lays down His bare word before us, as if saying, "Accept this because I say it," and for no other reason. Such a tone is unique, at least among sane teachers. There have been fanatics and self-deceived enthusiasts in abundance, who have clashed down their unsupported assertions before men, and insisted on their reception; but they have been overwhelmed by universal scorn, or by still more galling laughter. One Teacher alone has succeeded in persuading men that He had a right to speak thus, and been taken at His own valuation. The phenomenon is absolutely unique.

Contrast the authoritative ring of this doubled "Verily, verily," with the prophets' standing formula, "Thus saith the Lord." The loftiest of the inspired men who dwelt nearest the throne of the Ineffable, and were in fullest possession of the secret of the Lord, never ventured to obtrude or even to show their own personality, but hid themselves behind the word of which they were but the vehicles. Christ never uses their manner of speech, and seeks not, as they did, to secure acceptance for His utterances by tracing them to the Lord; but while He declares that He speaks that which He heard of the Father, He separates His manner of hearing from that of ordinary inspiration as much as He does His manner of communicating the thing heard from that of other organs of the Divine Word. "Thus saith the Lord" was the seal impressed on the prophetic word; "I say unto you" is the characteristic of Christ's. Thus He stands above the prophets, by whom at sundry times and in divers manners God spake unto men, being not only, as they were, messengers, but Himself the Message.

Contrast His authoritative teaching with that sort which

was in vogue in Palestine at the time. We are told that to understand Jesus we must study the rabbinical teaching of His day, in which we shall find the germs of His. That teaching is well worthy of study by competent persons, and affords much interesting material for the elucidation of the Gospels; but the verdict of the generation which heard both it and Jesus is nearer the truth than the modern idea that He was only a Rabbi of a better sort. The difference between Him and the doctors of the Law, not the likeness, was what struck the people who were familiar with both. "They were astonished at His doctrine: for He taught them as having authority, and not as the scribes." However little they apprehended the substance of His teaching, they felt the difference in its manner from that to which they were accustomed; and the difference lay precisely here, in the tone of authority with which He spoke. The rabbis and scribes founded their decisions on tradition, as any one who reads a page of the Talmud will see. Rabbi This says so-and-so; Rabbi That says thus. Rabbi A, in the name of Rabbi B, said this; and so on to weariness. They passed from one to another some stale drops of water drawn long ago by other hands. Jesus Christ stood forth among these retailers of other men's wisdom, from which any freshness that it ever had possessed had evaporated, as a fresh Fountain of certitude and truth, and "cried, saying, If any man thirst, let him come to Me, and drink." In His own Being are hidden the springs of wisdom and knowledge. His word is sovereign, and He has learned from no man. The contrast of His manner of teaching with that of the doctors His contemporaries is more important, and leads to truer conceptions of His nature and work than any fortuitous and isolated resemblances in specific sayings, which may be discovered, though these were more numerous and striking than they have yet been shown to be.

Contrast Christ's "Verily, verily," with the tone suitable to all thinkers who have learned the truths which they preach, and have come to apprehend them through meditation or study. It becomes them to argue. Christ asserts. The thinker shows the path by which he has cut his way through the tangled underwoods of error into the open where he sees the sky. Christ never speaks as if any previous ignorance or doubt had been His experience. He never traces His illumination to others. He never takes the place of a learner, either in the moment of speaking or in any previous time. He seldom or never supports His utterances by reasons, even although many of them are by no means self-evident or axiomatic. The virtues of all other servants and missionaries of truth, humility, self-oblivion, calm allegation of grounds for statements, acknowledgment of having grown by degrees to the apprehension of truth, are entirely absent in Jesus Christ. He clashes down His bare word before us, if we may so say, and bids us take it, simply and solely because it is His. As one of our old divines has it, "Man is problematical; Christ is dogmatical." And yet the world has recognized in this Teacher, who does the very things that would ruin any other teacher's reputation and influence, as the true "Master of those who know," and exalts Him as the Pattern and realized Ideal of what the guide of men should be. Strange that such an anomalous Master should have won such disciples! Stranger still that so many of them should so little understand the Master whom they profess to accept, as to be blind to the meaning of that anomaly in His method!

For if we once recognize this peculiarity in Christ's teachings, we should not stop till we have dealt fairly with the question, What right had Jesus to speak thus? Why should I take from His lips, on the authority of His bare word, what He chooses to say to me? By what title does He assume the place of a Teacher who has done all that is required of Him when He asserts? Surely there is but one answer possible to such questions. It cannot be too strongly stated or too often reiterated that the authority which He claims is unwarrantable usurpation unless He is "the Word of God." Unless we are prepared to accept Jesus as standing in an altogether different relation to the truth which He utters from that in which other men stand to those truths which they have attained to perceive, we cannot vindicate His method of teaching from the charge of arrogance, nor His character from a serious and well-nigh fatal flaw. But if it be the fact that He not merely apprehended, but was, the Truth, then we can understand His self-assertion, inasmuch as the self-manifestation of His personality is the fullest declaration and vindication of the Truth, which He is. Then, bowing before Him in whom the fulness of the wisdom of God did bodily dwell, and receiving Him as the Word who is the self-revelation of God and the Light of men, we learn the deep significance of His method. Only on the ground of His Divine authority is He vindicated from the charge of arrogant presumption, when instead of argument He gives Himself, and does not deign to commend His deepest and most mysterious utterances by any other reason for our acceptance of them than this, " Verily, verily, I say unto you."

II. Let me point out what this formula implies as to the certitude and importance of Christ's lessons.

"Verily, verily," is substantially equivalent to "Most certainly," and by its attachment to certain sayings of our Lord's, these are placed as in His estimation beyond cavil or hesitation. Other teachers have to say, "Peradventure," or "This I deem to be true;" but Jesus asserts, with unfaltering confidence, the irrefragable certitude and immovable stability of His utterances, and lays them down for the foundation of all our thinkings on the subjects which they touch.

In such a day as this, when all things seem to be cast into the cauldron again, and the firmest institutions and beliefs are melting away in the heat, the world needs, more perhaps than ever it did, to listen to that Voice, so calm and quiet, which yet rises clear above the hubbub of men, proclaiming their doubts or questionings, and speaks to us the ultimate and eternal truths on which mind, heart, and spirit can build, and, building, be at rest. Much is dark, much in organized institutions and written creeds is doubtful and perishable; but here at least is a central core of solid rock, which no pressure can cause to crumble nor any force shift: "Behold, I lay in Zion for a foundation a Stone, a tried Corner-Stone, a sure Foundation."

Think of the difference between the freshness and adaptation to the wants of this day, of the words of Jesus Christ, and the film of old-fashioned remoteness which has crept over all sayings of all the wise men of the past, except Himself, and tell us what is the secret of the immortal youth and close-fittingness of this Man's words. How happens it that to-day, amidst a world so different outwardly and inwardly from the simple life amid the Galilæan hills, where these words were first spoken, they come as close to us, and in many respects even closer than they did to those who heard them first? How happens it, except because they are so limpidly free from all admixture of the soil that there is nothing in them to decay, and hence all ages may drink and find them sparkling and fresh? Christ's words have no marks of human limitations, and therefore no fate of transitoriness, but are to every generation the basis of certitude. That sure foundation abides, like the massive blocks still to be seen in their places in the walls of Jerusalem, on which a hundred generations have looked as they passed into oblivion, and which still remain sharp-cut and solid as on the long-forgotten day when they were first laid. Christ's "Verily, verily," guarantees the absolute certainty of the truths which it heralds.

Further, this formula declares the importance of His teachings which are introduced by it. It calls special attention to these, and is, as it were, an underscoring of them, or printing them in italics. As I have already remarked, these truths are often by no means self-evident. On the contrary, the utterances to which Jesus attaches the double "Verily" are usually those which deal with most recondite and profound teachings.

A rough classification of the instances of the occurrence of the phrase, however imperfect it must necessarily be within our limits, may serve in some measure to bring out the importance of the truths commended to us by it. First, then, it points attention to teachings concerning Himself. With it He calls us to believe, on His authority, in His pre-existence: "Before Abraham was, I am." With it He asserts His unity of being and identity of action with the Father: "The Son can do nothing of Himself; but whatsoever things the Father doeth, these also doeth the Son likewise." He assumes the office of medium of all communication between earth and heaven: "Ye shall see the heavens open, and the angels of God ascending and descending upon the Son of man." He claims to be the means by which men enter the fold of God: "I am the Door of the sheep." He asserts that He is the infallible Teacher, speaking from personal experience of unseen things: "We speak that we do know, and testify that we have seen." He presents Himself as the God-given Source and Sustenance of true life: "My Father giveth you the true bread from heaven." He promises the certain acceptance of all prayer truly offered in His name: "Whatsoever ye shall ask of the Father in My name, He will do it." Finally, He proclaims that He must die in order to accomplish His life-giving purpose and mission: "Except a corn of wheat fall into the ground and die, it abideth alone: but if it die, it bringeth forth much fruit." So His Divine nature, pre-existence, absolute union of being and identity of action with the Father, His position and office as the Channel of all God's approach to us and of ours to Him, His infallible reading off to us of the things which He has seen and heard in the depths of eternity and the glories of the throne, and the solemn necessity for His death of shame, are all commended to us, not by argument, but simply by His "Verily, verily, I say unto you." These are not self-evident truths, but, recondite and mysterious as some of them are, Jesus brings nothing to support them but His own word. "Because He could swear by no greater, He sware by Himself."

A second set of His sayings thus prefaced refers to us and our relations to Him. Thus He reveals the condition of spiritual life as being union with Him by faith: "Except ye eat the flesh of the Son of man, and drink His blood, ye have no life in you;" "He that heareth My word, and believeth in Him that sent Me, hath everlasting life;" "If a man keep My sayings, he shall never see death." He asserts with the same strong confirmation the necessity of a new nature being communicated ere men can either see or enter the kingdom of God: "Except a man be born again, he cannot see the kingdom of God;" and again, "Except a man be born of water and of the Spirit, he cannot enter into the kingdom." With the same strong confirmation He presents Himself as the Pattern of lowly love and self-abasing service to all His followers: "The servant is not greater than his lord." He lovingly identifies Himself with us, and hints at a transcendent unity of being with Him: "He that receiveth whomsoever I send, receiveth Me." He even holds out the promise, that as He, in His mysterious oneness with the Father, did the same Divine works, so His servants, by virtue of their corresponding union with Him, shall exercise activities like His: "The works that I do shall he do also, and greater works than these shall He do."

There remain one or two other instances of the use of the double "Verily," which belong to less profound matters. It is sometimes employed in Christ's predictions, both of a near and of a remote future, which could only be made by supernatural knowledge, and must obviously be accepted on His bare word. "One of you shall betray Me;" "Ye shall weep and lament, . . . but your sorrow shall be turned into joy;" "The cock shall not crow till thou hast denied Me thrice;" "When thou wast young, thou girdedst thyself, . . . but when thou art old, another shall gird thee."

Still further, He employs the expression once or twice

when, with Divine penetration of insight and certitude of stroke, He lays bare to men their hidden foulness of nature, as when He says, "Ye seek Me, not because ye saw the miracle, but because ye did eat of the loaves;" or again, "He that doeth sin is the servant of sin."

So, in all the sayings to which this double "Verily" is attached, we can discern more or less clearly the appeal to His Divine authority as Revealer; and the most of them are truths which would never have dawned on men's minds except He had uttered them, but, being uttered, become the pillars of our faith and the core of the gospel.

III. Lastly, we have to consider what this form of confirmation implies as to the scholars.

It implies that those to whom it was addressed had dull ears, whose languid attention needed to be stimulated, or that the words were too great to be easily believed, or too unwelcome to be swiftly accepted. So it is a solemn warning against prejudice, apathy, and sloth; an exhortation to earnest attention and sharp-eared listening; an appeal to us to permit no indifference to come between us and His Word, nor to stop our ears with the clay of earthliness and sin against His gentle but authoritative voice.

Plainly, the course of our thoughts thus far leads to the conclusion that, since Christ is a Teacher thus authoritative, and His words are thus certain and important, our attitude as His scholars should be that of absolute submission. That which it is degradation to give to a man, it is sin to withhold from Christ. When men speak to us, we have the right and the obligation to say, "How do you know? Why should I believe you?" We have the right to question and to disagree. When Christ speaks, the only fit reply is, "Speak, Lord; for Thy servant heareth." Much is uncertain.

On this voice we may absolutely rely. None other is authoritative. Let us, then, silence all other voices, and let Him speak. Come to Christ for yourself, and for yourself hearken to, and take from Him at first-hand what He has to say to you. Thinkers, speculators, books, reviews, currents of opinion, the *Zeitgeist*, and the like, are poor substitutes for the supreme authority of the one Teacher, the Teacher of all truth, the Teacher for all generations. Do not take your conceptions of Him and His words at second-hand. Do not let your own wishes, or sentiments, or thinkings shape your creed. Listen to Jesus Christ, and what He says do you take into your inmost heart, and on it build all your beliefs.

The absolute certitude of His message has for its corresponding attitude our unwavering steadfastness. It seems to be thought a mark of "advanced Christianity" that we should not be sure as to any of its doctrines, but hold them all provisionally—as if such an attitude were possible. Provisional belief is practical unbelief. I do not wish any man to say, "I am sure," when he is not. Premature certainty ends in too late doubt. But whilst there will always be for us, in our beliefs, based on Christ's self-revelation, a circumference or horizon of darkness, there would be no circumference unless there were a centre, and no consciousness of the dark rim unless the centre were light. There will always be much about which we shall be wisest to say, "The Lord hath not showed it unto me." But that should not hinder us from firmly grasping the grand certainties, which we can without presumption affirm, and cannot without presumption deny, since Jesus has sealed them with His own attesting word. Let us not falter in adding our voices to the chorus of believers who take up the old triumphant words, "We know that the Son of God is come, and hath given us an understanding that we may know Him that is true." When Jesus speaks His "Verily, verily, I say unto you," let us add our "Amen" of acceptance to His "Verily" of assurance. Let us respond to His faithfulness with our faith, and build rock on the rock, and, turning to that gentle and infallible Teacher, the incarnate Truth, as our refuge from the jangle of controversies and the strife of tongues, let us humbly and resolvedly say to Him, "Lord, to whom shall we go? Thou hast the words of eternal life."

BIBLIOGRAPHY.

Spring Holiday in Italy. 1863. Palmer and Howe.

Sermons preached in Manchester. First Series, printed December, 1863 (Crown 8vo); Second Series, 1865 (Fcap. 8vo); Third Series, 1869. Reprinted 1871, 1874, 1875, 1877, 1879, 1881, 1883, 1887. Macmillan and Co.

Week-day Evening Addresses. 1877. Macmillan and Co.

Secret of Power, and other Sermons. 1882. Macmillan and Co.

Life of David as reflected in his Psalms. 1880. Hodder and Stoughton.

Colossians and Philemon (Expositor's Bible). 1887, 1888. Hodder and Stoughton.

A Year's Ministry. 1884. Christian Commonwealth Co.

Christ in the Heart. 1886. Christian Commonwealth Co.

The Unchanging Christ. 1889. Alexander and Shepheard.

The Holy of Holies. 1890. Alexander and Shepheard.

The God of the Amen. 1891. Alexander and Shepheard.

Notes on International Sunday School Lessons. American Sunday School Times, 1887–91.

www.ingramcontent.com/pod-product-compliance
Lightning Source LLC
Chambersburg PA
CBHW020901230426
43666CB00008B/1262